"AND LET THE CHURCH SAY, *AMEN!*"

A GUIDE TO BETTER COMMUNICATION, LOVE AND SEX

By: Sabrina Washington, RN BSN

First Edition: October 2021
Title: And Let the Church Say, Amen! A Guide to Better Communication, Love and Sex

Self-Published
Author: Sabrina Washington
Subjects: Romance, Christianity, Love & Marriage, Health

Library of Congress Control Number: 2021914624

Identifiers: ISBN 978-1-7371695-0-5 (Hardcover)
                978-1-7371695-1-2 (Paperback)
                978-1-7371695-2-9 (eBook)

Printed in the United States of America

Cover design by Aquib Awais

Acknowledgments

Writing this book seemed like an impossible task until something, or shall I say, someone, on the inside said, "You can do it." Thank You, Holy Spirit. Along this journey, there have been many people who've encouraged me to follow my aspirations and inspired me to hang-on in there despite the hardships I've faced. The scripture that says **what's impossible with man is possible with God,** Luke 18:27, rings true because when I was at my weakest point and didn't think I had any purpose, God came through. The hardest part was actually starting. And after that flame was lit, well, the rest is literally history. Here are the cheerleaders I'd like to thank:

God for keeping me in the eye of the storm, for His love and the daily internal prompts He gives to push through and get it done. God, you are my light and the reason I keep it all together. Without you, No-thing is possible.

Julius Washington Sr., my husband and my best friend, thank you for being my inspiration, without even knowing it. For your love, support and encouragement, especially when I wanted to throw in the towel.

Easter Cato, my mother and queen, you've inspired me never to give up in the face of adversity. You are a true gem, and I'm so eternally grateful for your love and continued support, I couldn't have done it without you.

Willie Cato Sr., my father who is with God now but who showed me every day how to be more, how to love and to be the very best version of myself.

Tanaka Cato, my sister; my rock, who is a powerful warrior for Christ and love of my life, thank you.

And my brother, Willie Cato, who signifies what is to be a man and father, thank you for always showing up.

And to all those who continue to fervently pray for me, encouraging me not to give up, to continue to run this race: My children, Dominique Rice (thank you so much for your contributions), DePaul Davis, Desirée Poole, the original cheerleaders who believed that I could and so I did, for supporting me every step of the way, I love you dearly. To Traci Washington, our eldest, thank you so much for your contribution to the cause, for your love and support, thank you. To Glyndelle Poole, thank you for your comments in the book, I love and appreciate you. Also, shout out to Desirée Poole for the inside photos.

To Julius Washington Jr. and Brittnei Washington, thank you for opening your hearts to me, I love you way more than you'll ever know.

To Dyllan & Dailee Davis (my teens) I want to be the very best example for you, to show you that nothing is impossible with God and that you can do anything you put your minds to. I love you! To the eight, I thank each of you for supporting me along the way. Shout out to Dailee Davis, who is 13, for the cosmetic tutorials for the cover design.

To my aunt, Dollie Henson, who's always filled my head and told me I could, thank you for believing in me. I love you. My cousin, Kia'ora Henson who told me many years ago to just write a little each day, even if it were a simple line, and before I knew it, I would have a book, thank you.

At the same time, I would like to thank everyone who had a part in this journey: Pastor Peete of Genesis Church, Jameka Rothschild for leading me to Marcello Bice (my coach and cheerleader), for giving me the tools, in the end, to make this book happen, you rock!

To my photographer, Zainab Mohamad, my book cover designer, Aqib Awais, my formatter Tariq Khan and my copy editor, Sarah Singer, thank you all so very much; you made this process easier.

Everybody needs someone in their lives to be better; that's the way God designed us, to love and encourage those around us to make them better. Ultimately, we love because He first loved us. 1 John 4:19

Dedication

———————⟨∞⟩———————

I dedicate this book to all of the women who feel less than. You can make it. I dedicate this book to every struggling couple who feels as if their marriage is lost. There's hope. I dedicate this book to the couples who feel as if they're on top but can't even sit in a room together behind closed doors. There's so much more to your relationship.

You see, God has allowed me to have an untainted love affair with the love of my life. To be in a relationship and feel love I never thought possible. I used to lay in bed at night with a saturated pillow and wonder to myself if I would ever experience true love. I somehow knew that love was possible because of how it felt on the inside, but for some reason, I just wasn't on the receiving end.

I've now lived and experienced the kind of love that God always desired for me to have. The love that warms the soul, makes you tingle where it counts and puts a smile on your face even during adversity. It's the kind of love that every woman and every man deserves to feel and have in their lifetime.

In addition, it's the kind of love that's endless as the wind. It never stops but continues from city to city, state to state, continent to continent, encapsulating you with a supercharge, allowing you to soar beyond your wildest dreams.

Foreword

———— ⌒◦∾◦⌒ ————

"And Let the Church Say, Amen!" a book long overdue but right on time for those who are willing and ready to stop pretending. Brother, you don't have it all together. Sister, your marriage isn't perfect. Yes, he was unfaithful and yes, there are intimacy issues. But these problems are often more prevalent than many are willing to share, even among the church. However, Sabrina Washington takes us all the way there.

In this book, you will follow her journey through a myriad of circumstances she has overcome. Each chapter incorporating the word of God, which she boldly proclaims and acknowledges as her daily strength. It is her relationship and obedience to Christ that birthed this book as she was aware there would be many who questioned, but God is more concerned about his people being healed. Sister you no longer have to hide your struggles or experiences. Brother, you are not alone. This book will touch the hearts of both men and women. There will be periods of laughter, you will be shocked, and you may even get teary eyed. But one thing is for sure, when it's all said and done you will say, "Let The Church Say, Amen!".

Tanaka Cato, BS, Deputy Probation Officer, Contra Costa County

What The Church Means to Me

Church has always been the cornerstone of my life, my go-to on the weekends and the congregational grounds on Sundays. Church has always been a joy in my life, a place I went to practice, learn and of course, Praise. When I think of Church, I automatically think of the building. Where I've spent more than 40 years of my life, performing rituals, singing songs, teaching our youth. It's where I drew my strength.

I spent so many years thinking that the church was a place that gave hope, a place that brought order and deliverance, a place for the weary and lost, but I was only partially right. Much to my surprise, I learned that the church wasn't the building (a "yeah-no" moment), but it was the residence of the heart. We, the people, are the church.

The Church: the people or followers of Christ are those who propel the word of God. The people, those who believe in God, are the ones who like Paul, Peter, James and John got the message out about hope, love and restoration to change the lives of people around the world.

So, what does church mean to me? Everything! Church, the internal dwelling place, church the building, church the foundation and instruction in my life, a call to order when chaos hits. Church is that reliable mainstay that never changes, a place of rest and new life happening every second of the day that you're linked to.

Joshua 24:15 – **But as for me and my house, we will serve the Lord**.

Church the place is something that is non-negotiable in our house, a learning mechanism by which growth happens and whereby lives are transformed. My life has truly been changed because of what I know, but more importantly, because of who I know. God is everything to me. He is my strength, my comfort, my peace, and it's because of Him that I live and have found my new place in life. And in the words of Erica Campbell, "I love God, you don't love God, what's wrong with you?"

Table of Contents

Whenever you see this symbol ☼- my husband has made a comment.

Chapter 1 – *Love Me*

My husband told me on our first date that after meeting me for the first time, he saw a snapshot of our relationship and wanted to be the best man in my movie; he's so smooth. As we sat there in the car, he then proceeded to play "Heaven Hooked Us Up" by The Isley Brothers. What he meant was that he wanted to have a permanent place in my life, to be a permanent fixture, so to speak.

Ten years later, he is literally the star in my book, the person of interest, the head of our home. Julius Washington is the man that God put in place to give me the kind of love I had never felt before and only dreamed of, the one who would lead our family and place God at the head where He so belongs. But he is so much more than that; he is a shoulder to cry on, the preacher/teacher of God's word, a wonderful father and friend, a comedian that doesn't have a filter or an off button and a fantastic lover. I mean, God really hooked me up, and my husband thought it was him, but I'm the one that came away with the winning ticket.

As I reflect on the sad yet painful experience of my previous marriage that came to an end a few months shy of 20 years, I thank God for blessing me with a teacher, preacher, father, friend, a lover, a comedian – a do-it-again, for real second time around kind of man. Every time I think of my husband and the incredible love I have for him, I find myself wrapped in a whirlwind, falling more in love with him and giving God all the praise for the miracle he orchestrated in our lives.

The crazy thing about our relationship is that both of our hearts had been broken. Our bodies and spirits had been trampled on and kicked to the curb, and we now wore the badge labeled, "Battered and Scarred." What we didn't know then but know now was that God was setting us up for a blessing and complete restoration. The two of us being united was and is like a new birth taking place, perfect and whole, ready to take on the challenges and beauty of life.

My husband sometimes tells a story during his sermons of a hunk of clay that was sitting in the corner and not pleasing to the eye. The potter put the clay on the potter's wheel, and when the clay first felt the wheel, it was cold and uncomfortable. The clay told the potter how he felt, and the potter said, "Don't worry, you'll be fine." The potter started pulling the imperfections out of him, probing, stretching and molding him.

The clay told the potter, "Hey! This is uncomfortable." The potter's response was, "Don't worry, you'll be fine." Then the potter doused him with water, and the clay felt as if he was drowning. "Hey! Are you trying to kill me?" asked the clay. The potter said, "Don't worry, you'll be fine." Then the wheel started spinning and the clay started getting dizzy and close to nausea. He again told the potter his symptoms. And again, the potter told him, "Don't worry, you'll be okay."

Then, after this process, he looked in the mirror, and he thought to himself, "Wow! I look better than before." He was of course referring to being in a dark corner and just a lump of clay. Then the potter placed him in the oven, and he thought he would burn to death. "Hey! It's hot in here. I'm going to burn to death," the clay said. The potter's response was, "Trust me, you will be fine." The potter took him out of the oven, placed him on the table and started to paint him with different colors, and the fumes of the paint started to make him cough and feel uncomfortable. "I can barely breathe here," the clay said. Of course, the potter's response was, "You are going to be fine."

Just when he thought it was all over, the potter placed him in the oven again, but this time, the oven was twice as hot. "OMG! You're really trying to kill me, I'm sure of it," the clay said. The potter's response was, "You're going to be alright." Then the potter took him out of the oven and placed him on the top shelf in his store, and people came from all around and admired the now-teapot, it was the most beautiful pot in the store. People came in and wanted to purchase the teapot, but the potter's response was, "It is only for display, this one belongs to me."

The point of this story, as it relates to our marriage, was that God had to take us through many uncomfortable and painful experiences in our lives to allow us to be stronger and ready to handle the things ahead. God prepared us for each other, this union called marriage that He had predestined for us. That's what God did for us. He put the building blocks in place and then took us on a guided tour called life. What He did was set us up for the ultimate love experience that either of us was expecting. Mind-blowing! God is truly amazing!

When I met love, it wasn't just Love the feeling or Love the look. It was Love the person who was the epitome of Love that breathes life into all those around it. Love without a doubt gives and grinds and sometimes feels as if it's drowning, but you see, Love survives, Love wins. True love is never overshadowed and is always fragrant to the very end.

I've learned over the years that if any relationship is going to last, it's important to know your partner intimately.

And if you want to keep the relationship sizzling, way before the bedroom, get to know their innermost thoughts and desires. To take it a step further, find out the precise area(s) on the body that turn them on to the point of exhilaration, and still, I'm not talking about intercourse – not yet anyway.

If you want your relationship to move forward, it's necessary for both individuals to be open and honest and not afraid to spill the beans. Partners, you also have to be non-judgmental, practice good listening skills, ask questions to ensure your understanding, make sure you validate them and be open to change. Be the change for the growth and development of the relationship.

When you're in the exploration phase of your relationship (the newbies), it's important to understand that during this stage in the relationship, it's merely superficial. You can't possibly think you know the other person after a few dates, weeks or even months. Please know that it's highly probable that one, if not both of you, at some point during this phase are wearing masks (and not because of COVID19).

The exploration must continue; do research, unwrap all the layers to see who you really have in front of you. Have numerous calls during the days and nights, frequent dates, hold hands, kiss, giggle... just have organic fun. It's these things that determine if the relationship will go to the next level and find Love. Likewise, it is precisely these things that will be necessary to keep the relationship going and help it remain whole. If this does not sound like your current relationship, it may be fair to say that one or both of you stopped making an effort or finding time for each other along the way (what may seem to be ages ago), but just know that YOU CAN GET IT BACK. Both of you just need to be willing to put in the work.

What Made Me Write This Book

My husband fulfilled me even before we had intercourse; he's a bad man, and by bad, I mean damn good. He completely rocked my being. This man I now call my husband is the love of my life. He is a blessing from the Most-High God, who I thank every day that I wake up and have breath.

You see, before my husband came into my life, I was dying emotionally, I was done. I was over 40, lonely, lost, and depressed. I had five kids, three of whom were shattered by the divorce, a good job as a Director of Nursing, which seemed to be one of the only good things going for me at the time, but I was also going through a nasty divorce. I had come to the realization that I may never be happy; I didn't know my worth, and I was spiritually exhausted, but God! **(He heals those who have broken hearts. He takes care of their wounds.** Psalms 147:3 NIRV).

I had been in a 20-year relationship, and we missed the mark when it came to making it work. In my opinion, we were just too young when we started out, not knowing enough about who we were and what was necessary to make the relationship work. With all of the information I now possess, or shall I say, lessons of LIFE: (Learning, Invaluable, Fundamental, Experiences), I now know that the image of marriage that society gives is not a realistic one.

To have a successful union, there are things you should understand, and valuable tools you need to gain in order for the relationship to work well. What's clear is that a couple starting out must have a role model: a successful marriage or image modeled or drawn from. Are you able to decipher what a successful marriage looks like? Are you getting married for the right reasons? Did you tie the knot because of love or something else?

At the same time, are you on the same page when it comes to core values? What role does religion play in your lives and hence the impending marriage? And lastly, how do you view intimacy, sex, family, kids, etc.? These are just some of the necessary questions that should be answered before you say, "I DO." And if you've already married, see if the two of you are aligned when it comes to the above. (If you don't seem connected, you've got your work cut out for you. Keep reading).

It is my deepest desire that married couples stay connected emotionally and physically without allowing any distractions to wreak havoc on their relationship. Understanding who you are and *whose* you are is key. The reality is that God wants the very best for us and that sexual desire for one another is natural; it is how we love and is directly given from Him.

The average person doesn't read the Bible for understanding, but if you do, it will literally, blow your mind. A relationship or a connection with one another is what God wants from us: pure, unfiltered and free, no strings attached. Free to explore your desires and expectations with your partner so that there are no outside forces.

To put it plainly, no stepping-out or extramarital affairs because if you're honest with yourself and your spouse, all of your needs will be met, and the relationship will be stronger than ever, lacking nothing. Furthermore, you will find amazing gratification in the process. I pray that you find enjoyment in life with your spouse and that this book gives life and inspiration to your relationship.

I'm certain that if you use these tools, advice and strategies, coupled with God's word, *No Thing* will be able to come between you two. Oh! And the sex, yes sex, it is the magic wand that God gave to us for fulfillment and to abracadabra away the natural stressors that are placed on every relationship. Sex is also one of the necessary tools to keep the attraction going. The Bible *does* say to do it often, it sure does, so why not give it your all and do it well. ☼ (1 Corinthians 5:7, **Do not deprive each other except perhaps by mutual consent and for a time, so that you may devote yourselves to prayer. Then come together again so that Satan will not tempt you because of your lack of self-control.**) God gave your partner to you so that you can indulge... Have your cake and eat it too!

It's so important to take the time and find out what brings you joy in your relationship when it comes to making love and to ask your partner or spouse to do the same. Don't be afraid or ashamed to talk about sex and the experience it yields. If the Bible does, shouldn't you? If you want him to say your name, say your name, you owe it to yourselves to do an in-depth exploration of each other's minds and bodies. You will be quite surprised when you put aside all the things you've heard in the past about sex that have a negative connotation.

When you think of sex and the satisfaction we get from it, it seems almost forbidden to discuss it in the church or amongst its members, as if God were going to get you for enjoying it. Intimacy and sex should be a regular discussion in the church, teaching its members how to love their spouse, sex, and the beauty of it, as well as what premarital sex looks like and why we should avoid it. Furthermore, we should encourage teachings on the different kinds of love and what people should look for or expect as a way to keep their marriages alive and in shape.

Why Is Discussing Sex Taboo?

I had to ask myself this same question and figure out why it initially made me feel uncomfortable talking about sex to my children. The answer for me was that intimacy and/or intercourse wasn't discussed in my home when I was growing up. Furthermore, the sex educational topics in school brought a lot of giggles and side conversations and therefore left me with some knowledge but lacking the full extent of what it really meant. It was important for me as a parent to answer any questions and destroy myths so that my children got the truth at home instead of being led astray when the conversations happened around their peers.

How I started the conversation was a blessing in disguise.

It was back when my first group of kids were young. My first group of children are 33, 30 and 28, while the second group are 13 and 12. I was definitely going through a mid-life crisis to get my tubes untied when my youngest was 15 and start all over again. Deep inside I believed that having another child would fix any problem in my marriage – boy, was I wrong.

Back then, I used to have many kids in my home, and it was completely not unusual to have three or four extra kids over each weekend. One day, I was upstairs in my bedroom with the window open because the kids were in the backyard when I heard one of them say, "I had sex." Did my mom ears deceive me or did those young kids, none of them over 12, say what I thought they said?

Yep, I heard it, so I called everyone upstairs, had them stand in a circle and I told them what I heard and then had each of them tell me what sex was. Horrified, their eyes were as wide as saucers, but each of them knew they had to say something because "I don't know" wasn't an option for me. None of them had it right (praise be to Jesus). I heard everything from holding hands to kissing to humping. The short version of the conversation was me telling them that sex was something that shouldn't come out of the mouths of a child and that no one should touch their private parts, but if anyone attempted to, they should tell an adult immediately.

At the same time, sex was something beautiful that was shared by a husband and wife, a man and a woman. Furthermore, that sex was not dirty and definitely not a secret act, but that it was gifted by God, for two people to share and love each other, again, not by kids. My best friend was not a happy camper with me when she heard what I'd told her child, but I told her that either they were going to get the information from someone they could trust or learn it on the street from someone who was just as ignorant as themselves.

Kids need to hear the truth from their parents, a trusted source. Another funny story was when one of my kids from my second group (my daughter, 11 at the time) told my husband and me, at the breakfast table, that we kept her up all night. I could have died right there at the table. She added, "I thought you were dying because you were screaming." Oh my goodness, I wanted to disappear. My first response was to laugh, then I calmly said, "Well, if you thought I was dying, what changed your mind?" She replied, "I got up, and then I heard Julius cussing, and I knew then that you weren't dying." After I regained my composure, we were able to have a real conversation about life. I told her that married couples make love, they have sex, and that I was sorry for scaring her and we would be mindful to keep it down next time. (Xfinity, Music Channel is our go-to when the mood is right because there is absolutely no way I can be quiet.)

So, the question still remains, why are we ashamed to talk about the way we feel or about the mere fact that our bodies were created out of love to love? Love is a pure and natural act that was never meant to be hushed or symbolized, or to become a stagnant, repetitive act. The art of making love, having sex, intercourse, mating, procreation (or whatever you call it) was meant to be shared among a man and a woman, and this act was meant to be blissful, yep! Pure pleasure, and it all started in the Bible. For those who aren't familiar with it, it all began in the first book of the Bible, Genesis. God created the first woman because He didn't want man to be alone. God's creation of humans was so that they would unite and love one another from head to toe. He created the wo-man to be the helpmeet that was necessary to propel the world. But there's more to it than that, right? Let's go a bit deeper. This union was created by God, for the two to love one another and respect one another (mentally and physically). They (Adam and Eve) were initially at peace with themselves and their bare bodies.

One can only assume or imagine the various mention of adjectives Adam may have used when he saw Eve's body for the first time, without any element of deception. I mean, it was Adam who named every creature on earth, the authority was given to him, so can you envision it? I can imagine him saying, "Dam girl, you fine, a beautiful work of art!" I'm sure Adam was thanking God; praising His holy name when he saw her and giving a shout of praise each and every time he made love to her.

Well, let us go to Song of Solomon and take a closer look at the words of Solomon (son of King David), the writer of this book, and see how colorful his view is on love. If you're not familiar with Solomon, well, he was one of the original masterminds; he was very eloquent, and he must have been a phenomenal lover because he had 700 wives and 300 chicks on the side. I guess you could call Solomon a player from the Himalayas!

He was one of the wisest men, says God, and he knew how and when to say just the right thing, I believe that is why God chose him to be an example to us, to know how to seductively talk to our mate and feel good about it. All out of love.

Song of Solomon 1:10 NIV, **your cheeks are beautiful with earrings, your neck with strings of jewels.**

Let's Take a Closer Look

Right here, he's checking her out and giving her compliments. Men, you can learn something from this. Notice your women and tell her how beautiful she is, not when you want to get some but just because you should. Now for my ladies, it doesn't hurt to tell him how scrumptious he looks. It really is a stroke to the ego that we could all use here and there. If hygiene or looks leave something to be desired, then find those soft words of encouragement to throw at him or her.

If you know what you like, then share it because what we want is for our mates to look and desire us and vice versa. It's really no different than going on a series of first dates when we look and smell our best. We step up the grooming game and put our best foot forward because we want our date to see the best image of ourselves. This is an ongoing thing and even though the years bring comfort or lackcisicty (yep, I made that up) in the way we look and behave, it shouldn't be a way of life.

Listen! Things that are thriving in life, whether it's the human body, animals or even plants, it is because we take care of and nurture them. Well, all I'm saying is that we should maintain our own body image and that of our relationships. If he's not looking at you, trust me, he will be looking at someone else that catches his eye. And the truth of the matter is that men and women do admire the opposite sex for their beauty because they have it all together on the surface, so shouldn't we keep it together for our man or mate?

Song of Solomon 1:13 NIV, **My beloved is to me a sachet of myrrh resting between my breasts. MSG, When my king-lover lay down beside me, my fragrance filled the room. His head resting between my breasts — the head of my lover was a sachet of sweet myrrh. My beloved is a bouquet of wildflowers picked just for me from the fields of Engedi.**

Women, what do you see here? Not only should we look good enough to eat, but he should smell that sweet aroma coming from our heated bodies. The senses are extremely powerful, and we not only use our eyes as an attractive mechanism but our noses as well. You see, when we make love, we don't only do it with our genitals. All that God has given us should be used. If you haven't been using all of your senses, then start, because you're missing out.

Chapter 2 - *Preamble to Sex*

Wonders of the Senses

Just as a brush-up, there are five senses: sight, sound, smell, taste, and touch, that when ignited or engaged send signals from that sensory organ to the brain telling the body if we like what we are sensing or not. When we think of making love, we may think that touch is the only sense we need to make a thing go right, but in reality, we need them all to truly achieve long-lasting fulfillment.

Now, I'm not saying that a quickie every now and again isn't awesome, but if you want to have those memories, the kinds that curl your toes, then engage all the senses.

Sight: What your partner sees is often the first trigger in them being aroused.

Explore his or her image of sexy, what turns them on. Women, if you're comfortable in sweats and a t-shirt, try changing the baggy pants to fitted ones and a fitted t-shirt without a bra. At the same time, try going to bed in comfortable yet sexy nightclothes, like a silky gown with mesh combination or a fitted shorts and t-shirt combination. And men, make sure your grooming is on point because women love a clean, groomed man, or shall I say, most do.

Sound: It's said that women express themselves more during sex; however, this isn't our story. My husband does more talking than a Baptist preacher. Oh right – he is a preacher! But ladies, if you're not a talker, that's quite alright. Learn to express yourselves through meaningful sounds and groans.

Honey child, let it rip, I'm here to tell you that those sounds enhance the whole sexual experience, making you feel it where it counts, on the inside. At the same time, try some soothing music or whichever you both agree on to get you in the mood. Remember, communication is the key; tell your partner what turns you on or what feels good (or not) as they stroke your body and vice versa.

Smell: The nose has the ability to either turn you on or all the way off. Smell plays a more important role in sex than you might think. (Hmm, am I going to insert this? Yep!) My husband is turned on by the smell of the mighty "V," not to mention the taste. He loves it. I guess I can't leave myself out this conversation. I simply love his penis (church folk, yes, I said penis. It is its anatomical name, right?), the way it looks, feels and tastes, I know God made it just for me.

Well, let us take a closer look at why we feel this way. Pheromones! Pheromones are chemicals produced in our bodies that are excreted in our perspiration, urine, and in the penis and vagina. They influence how we feel about a mate and drive our sexual behavior. Pheromones work on a subconscious level. You don't notice the smell, but you feel the effects, which can include:

- Being more sexually attractive to the opposite sex
- Increased confidence
- More passion in the bedroom
- Making the opposite sex more comfortable around you
- More respect from members of the same sex

Touch: Touch is a vital part of communication, physical health, and wellbeing. We learn early on how important human touch is to the newborn development. Touch soothes, it calms nerves, it bonds the mother and baby and sends signals of love, not to mention allowing the child to thrive. Touch, at the same time, is an instrumental part of achieving great sex. Women, if your man goes straight for the "V" push that stick back and tell him what you desire, exactly what you need. To figure out where your pleasure points or zones are, take sex off the table, just for a short time (calm all the way down, it's not forever) and begin to explore each other's bodies.

I know you may be thinking, "How can I go without sex?" but if we're talking orgasms, well, those can also be achieved during touch without penetration. Take some needed time to explore. I personally like the back of my neck, earlobes, and the center of my back rubbed, licked, or lightly touched. If you're struggling with how you may fit this into your busy schedules, you can replace TV time prior to bed with Exploration Time. To get him into it, tell him it's a game of head-to-toe with no exclusions and the goal being bliss.

Taste: Partaking in fellatio sends my body into overdrive, wanting to have sex immediately. At the same time, our taste buds are so sensitive that they can easily send positive and/or negative messages to the brain. One repulsive taste can also send you to the toilet before you know it, so keep it fresh. Have fun and let your tongue explore by trying flavored lubricants during oral indulgence; there are many options out there to discover. At the same time, you can try different kinds of fruits, puddings, chocolate, or whipped cream before kissing or licking your partner's gems. *Only for the outer surface, people. Never to be inserted. You don't want to get a bacterial or yeast infection.

Now let's explore more of what makes us feel good and the places on the body that elicit a favorable response. This leads us to the **Erogenous Zones**. This reminds me of a title of one of Dr. Suess' books, *Oh, the Places You'll Go!* Meaning, if you put forth the effort, enjoyment is literally on the horizon.

Touch Me, Feel Me, Taste Me – The Erogenous Zones

Erogenous zones – what are they and how do they fit into this discussion? To start, Merriam-Webster defines an erogenous zone as "a sensitive area on the body that causes sexual arousal when it is touched." Of course, we all know that the genital areas are sensitive, but some may not know that there are other areas on the body that elicit a sexual response, so let's explore this further. This diagram gives a simple view of where these areas are located.

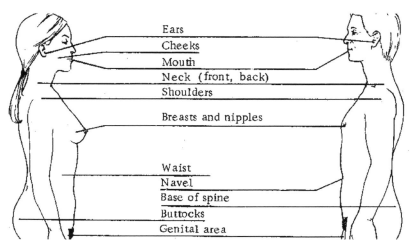

Ears
Cheeks
Mouth
Neck (front, back)
Shoulders
Breasts and nipples
Waist
Navel
Base of spine
Buttocks
Genital area

Source: Professorwill.blogspot.com

It's not on this diagram, but you can also try the scalp; it is very vascular and is loaded with many nerve endings that are sensitive to touch. At the same time, the back for some may trigger excitation. I love, love when my husband takes his wet tongue and licks the center of my back, it just does some *things* to me. I also love the inner thigh and outer labia, OMG!!! Whenever he strokes these places with his tongue, it literally sends chills up and down my spine.

The takeaway here is to explore every body part and see how your mate is affected by your touch. Just remember to be gentle, use light pressure and the closer you get to the genital area, the more aroused you will become. Hallelujah! Let the Church Say, Amen!

Goal: touch = *tingle* = pleasure!

Foreplay

Foreplay is essential, so if it's not happening in or out of the bedroom, get with it! If by chance you're not too sure how to accomplish foreplay, keep reading. For me, foreplay starts when he fills my head with expressive words, and not just before making love but, throughout the day or the week. I don't just want to hear how much he loves me right before I'm penetrated with his love. I want to not only hear it, but I want to feel it, see it in our lives, and see the love radiate all over him. Before my husband even touches me, I need to feel his love. In other words, the process of foreplay is ongoing.

You should start your day out by thanking God and then loving on the one He gave you. Because this is a normal occurrence in our relationship, I'm almost always guaranteed fireworks or a marvelous happy ending when we make love. I mean, orgasmic combustion is sure to be on the horizon, like a cataclysmic event. Because we (ladies) need emotional fillers along the way, I can honestly say that I play back his words spoken in my ear, the seductive glances, the wet kisses, and the erotic touches. I love it.

All of it matters when trying to achieve an orgasm, especially for the older woman (or maybe I'm just speaking for myself). If you, like me, struggle with health issues, sex can be a challenge; we literally may need an additional push. At the same time, as we age, many people face or struggle with decreased sexual arousal and become frustrated and stop attempting sex altogether. But I can say that love-making can be successful if you put in the time and effort; you must put in the work if you want a positive outcome. We will explore this later, so keep reading.

Now for the men, well, they sometimes have a lot to say, but what it literally boils down to with them is a visual field. Men are turned on by what they see, so it is important here to check yourselves out; do a self-evaluation. Whether the treat the eye finds delight in is physically present on their phone, their computer or television, what men want is an appetizer or quick fix to get them in the mood. Men, unlike us women, don't need much for eroticism to happen. They literally need to see and/or imagine the goodies to make the rise take place. ☼ It won't hurt to let him have a few sexy pictures of you on his phone.

For those who still can't grasp foreplay, according to Wikipedia, "Foreplay is a set of emotionally and physically intimate acts between... people meant to create sexual arousal and desire for sexual activity. Although foreplay is typically understood as physical sexual activity, nonphysical activities, such as mental or verbal acts, may in some contexts be foreplay. Foreplay can mean different things to different people."

I love this definition because it gives the reader clear insight into intimacy before the bedroom. It is my experience that in order for love-making to be meaningful, you need to remove the handcuffs and limitations that society, family, and ideals place on relationships. Foreplay, before the play or before the actual act, is using everything God gave you, your mind, eyes, ears, nose, tongue (oh yes, I love using the tongue), your hands, legs, of course, sex organs and even your feet. I mean, when it's good, it makes my toes do a dance. If you have never had this experience, well keep reading because details are a-coming.

An example of awesome foreplay may look like this: When you wake up, instead of rushing out of bed, take the time to greet your mate, look into his or her eyes and have a simple conversation while caressing their body. The goal is for your mate to remember the deposits you've made along the way; you want your love account to be in the positive as much as possible. If you've been allowed to see another day, then do yourself a favor and show gratitude and be excited for the new day that God has given you. This means being thankful for everything, leaving nothing out, including that hunk or pretty young thing lying across from you. If you're pressed for time, scoot or roll over and give him a sensual kiss.

I know morning breath is a thing, and for some, it is a turn-off, so if that's the case, you can still take part in and find ways to express love. Simply give them a tender kiss on the cheek, neck, ears (any erogenous zone), look into his or her eyes and tell them how deeply in love you are with them. If you have more time and are thinking "Ok, I'm feeling this," take it a step further and kiss his love stick or her honey pot or stroke it gently before getting out of bed.

Yes, I said it, and for those of you who are appalled, lighten up, because God's intention was for us to embrace our mate and have fun doing it; nothing should ever be off-limits when it comes to your spouse. Just remember that God gave you this man or woman to love freely, so there's no need to feel embarrassed or yucky about it; yes, I said "yucky."

When I think of sex or the act of making love, I get all tingly inside and am reminded of how blessed I am to have a man who is strong yet tender, a man who loves me without words, with an exaggerated act of expression. My husband simply goes beyond and back again to ensure that all my needs are met, and I love him for it. What do I mean by this? Simple communication goes a long way. My husband says that his foreplay begins much earlier than mine does. According to him, a few of his triggers are seeing me get in or out of the tub or glancing at my "Bedroom Candy," as he calls it (sexy, matching underwear) before I slip into my clothes.

After we got married, I remember him taking me to Victoria's Secret, or as he likes to call the store, "Vickie's" (he was paying, and I was along for the ride). As we walked around the store, we compared notes, he showed me what he liked, and I did the same. I then got measured for the correct size bras and styles that fit me (ladies, please know that if you've lost or gained weight, had children or if you're getting better with age, like myself, you need to get measured every couple of years because things move, drop and flop... "Jesus. why?"). And then, well, he bought me my first two sets of matching lingerie (I was 41 at the time). I felt like a big girl that had graduated into a new society. I was now in the Victoria's Secret club, alright!

Before this trip to Vickie's, I had never been with a man that wanted to visualize my goodies before, on or off, during intercourse or just casually walking around (or let's just say it was never communicated to me). To put myself out there, my mother had always bought my underwear (yes, my mamma). My husband and I to this day still chuckle when he refers to my then "granny panties." He has no filter and tells it like he sees it; he calls it being brutally honest.

My mother knew my size and how much I hated shopping, and every now and again she would buy me the full coverage bras and panties (you all know exactly which kind I'm referring to), some plain, some with polka dots or zebra stripes, but always full coverage. Mamma's underwear was so comfy, not to mention free, so I put them on with pride, now only a vivid memory because they've all been replaced by Vickie's.

So, let's continue with the subject at hand, foreplay. My husband has mentioned that foreplay for him happens after I get out of the bath or shower. And ladies trust, he is always looking; my man is a hawk, I can't get anything past him. There are times when we're in bed for the evening and he says, "I like that pink number you have on." In my head, I'm wondering how on earth did he see what I was wearing, I didn't see him anywhere around when I put them on?

All I can say is that our panties and bras do matter, and when we're not paying them any mind, like my granny use to say, the eagle is always watching. I had to learn this for myself (as a mature woman), but it's never too late to understand that lingerie stores are there for a reason. Like John Witherspoon use to say, "You've Got to Coordinate."

And if this next statement doesn't apply to you then disregard it, but Sista's, we have to keep it tight. Not just for our partner, but we should get in shape and stay fit for ourselves, for our own physical health. At the same time, get used to the mirror and learn to love what you see if you don't already. So how does this apply to foreplay? Well, if you don't like the image of yourselves and then you wear it like a garment, how on earth can you expect him to view you as anything other than the distorted image he sees through your eyes? Body image or a strong mental self-image of ourselves gives us the confidence it takes to delve into a stronger sexual relationship, hence allowing us to demonstrate or participate in foreplay without worrying if he will like what we have on or if he thinks we're fat, etc. If we love who we see and are strong in our beliefs about our bodies, then he will love it too!

So, put it on, a strong positive self-image of yourselves – it looks good on you. Build the best vocabulary for yourself and say or shout out those adjectives about yourself while glancing in that mirror: I am beautiful, I am confident, fearless, passionate, strong, provocative, etc. Learn to love the body you're in, no negativity allowed. My husband has been teaching me this from day one, and all I can say is, I'm getting better.

Start the day off right, each and every day with God's word, those words of affirmation followed by physical activity. Positive thinking turns into a more positive way of life and wellbeing. Psalms 139:14 says, **We are fearfully and wonderfully made by Him**. So, if we want to be here for a while, then we need to start taking care of the bodies God gave us.

You see when we feel good about ourselves, whatever the size or shape, we act differently. When we like what we see, we tend to be more self-confident and that translates into how we act and how our mate sees and views us.

When I say keep it tight, more plainly put, get your health together because you only have one body and if you want it to take care of you when you reach that golden age, then you'd better get a move on and take care of it. From a nurse's perspective, heart disease, along with many other conditions, starts when you're younger. This might not be true of all cases, but many disease processes start because we're non-compliant with our health.

After you've made that commitment, next take an inventory of your cabinets and refrigerator and get all (ok, most) of the processed foods out of there. (I love my bacon, so moderation is everything). At the same time, get those bodies moving with at least 20-30 minutes of cardiovascular activity each day. Start slow if this is new to you with just 5-10 minutes of motion and remember to talk to your doctor prior to starting anything new – no one knows your medical conditions better than you and your doctor. And please don't just fix you but make it a family affair, getting your spouse and kids to take part in their health as well; you're more likely to be successful working as a team, so do it together.

Trust me, when you're trying to go the long haul and make love happen, you don't want him or her pooping out too early, so take advantage of getting those bodies in shape for all things to *come*, literally – you'll catch that in a minute.

Earlier I mentioned foreplay as also being an emotional act, so throughout your day make sure you stay in contact and check in with one another. In the earlier part of our relationship, my husband would make it a point to call me from a different city. "I'm in the beautiful city of Santa Rosa, it's bright with a zero chance of rain," was his opening (he's a retired truck driver and I'm a disabled/retired nurse) and then the line I anxiously waited for was when he told me he loved me. My whole face would light up as if it were the first time he said it; this was a daily occurrence and it made me feel amazing inside.

Now, if you're in a position where you can't receive calls, you can still stay in touch by writing a short note and placing it in their lunch tote, purse or wallet (wrapped in their debit card to ensure they see it) or slipping a note in the pocket of their clothing. If none of these works for you, there's always the cell phone that everyone has. Send a captivating text message that drops their jaw, letting them know how you're going to make love to them the next time you see them. Keep it fresh and always new (remember your dating days and draw from them).

Never let a day go by without affirming your love for one another. Remember that tomorrow is not promised to any of us, so live each day as if it were your last. Hearing the words "I love you" feels good, sure, but some don't understand that love is actually an action word; therefore, it's not enough to just say the words all the time; know that *love* is felt most when it's demonstrated. A perfect example of love demonstrated is Christ: the agony He underwent and ultimately dying on the cross, and why, pray tell? It is because He loved us so much that He was willing to endure a horrendous death to bring us back in alignment with God, thus giving us life eternally.

The point I'm trying to drill home is that love is a sacrifice, love is work and it requires constant motion. And love, *if* exemplified correctly, will also bring those who participate in it an expected end: hope, peace, joy and confidence in the union. We will delve into what love means again later in the book.

Yes, we're still discussing foreplay. Why? Because it's the catalyst for amazing sex. According to Women's Health, "foreplay is the act of engaging throughout the day, it is the realm of kissing, touching and oral pleasure. Sex and intimacy are more than what is done in the bedroom, it's about what we see, taste, touch and hear. It is a journey, not a destination." Good stuff, Women's Health.

Foreplay is a demonstration of love that's felt with or without actual touch; now, you know that he's good when you have that sensual feeling all over your body and he hasn't even touched you yet – ooh wee, is my response to that! When you use it in this way, the act of love-making is something that some only dream about, let alone talk about. When you take your time and allow your whole self to be involved in the process, you will almost always have to hold off the explosion! Making love, although it seems to be a simple act, is so much more than insertion (more than wham bam, thank you ma'am), it takes time, so set it up right.

There is a process in all things, right? In the beginning, there was a process when God created the earth and then man. God took his calculated time and captured the perfect scenario before bringing man into the equation. At the same time, in order for your relationship to function at an optimal level, you actually have to do the work, so give it a fighting chance and put these practices into action.

Now, there are times when you have to take more time, so let's talk about some of those instances. When we meet individuals and think they're the perfect match for us and then get to know them and think, what the hell was I thinking? And unfortunately, there are other times when we get ourselves into a relationship and find out years later that the person we linked ourselves with was ALL WRONG for us and wasted years of our lives that we will never get back.

Well, take it from me, it's never too late to find the love God has for you. Additionally, if the love (or lack thereof) in your relationship appears to have died, or maybe the wick is burning low, **pray** and start anew (pray with your partner, ensuring that you're on the same page). Seeking Godly counsel should always be factored into the equation if you want your relationship to last. Take your hands off and allow God to lead you. If this man or woman was sent by God, well then you need to get to work and repair the damaged parts. Matthew 6:33 says, **Seek Him first and all His righteousness and all things will be given to you.**

Who Are You?

This is critical: before you think about having sex, take the time to pull back the layers and see who you are and what you're working with. Making love and allowing love with intensity to last, in my opinion, begins with an in-depth knowledge of each other. Take the time to get to know one another before sex is factored in. Is your attraction focused on your mate? Are they real or are they Memorex? Can you remove sex from the relationship and keep the passion, the love and the fun that a new relationship comes with? These seem like simple questions, right? But there is still another question you may want to ask yourself.

Ask yourselves, did God bring the two of you together? Whoa, now that's food for thought! I'll ask again, did God bring the two of you together? If you're not sure and not hitched yet, *STOP,* hold up, wait a minute! Pump your breaks and talk to Him – Him meaning God. See where you are in this stage of your life and how you possibly got there. Are you seeking something that cannot be achieved in your current relationship? If so, start with a relationship with God, and find *you* in the process. Get to know God and how *you* fit in this world we are all so desperately trying to be a part of. I read this quote not long ago in my Bible app, You Version:

"God's not looking at what we can do, He's looking at who we are in Him. Everything you do means nothing if you don't start at the foot of the cross empty-handed. Do we truly know Him?"

Once you've got those questions answered, then you will be able to get back on track with loving your mate the way God intended, and by loving, I don't mean intercourse, coitus, procreation etc. If you don't love yourself, then there is not a chance in hell that you can love your mate with an unselfish kind of love (Agape) that God intends.

As a side note, I heard a sermon from T.D. Jakes a short time ago, entitled "How to Get Your Fight Back." What caught my attention was when he said, "Stop trying to connect with people you don't fit with... The fact that it doesn't fit means that it's not a good fit for you... When you find the bone that fits with you, you don't have to work so hard. Stop trying to force what doesn't work."

This made me self-reflect on my past relationship because many times I tried to make it work when it was never God's intention in the first place. I can say that because it was me that wanted the relationship to work; I never sought God's advice or waited on Him to lead me. I guess I just didn't know how to seek God in this way, not to mention me being too young and immature to be entering into a heavy relationship called marriage. Wisdom will definitely teach you some things.

Let me be very clear, by no means am I telling any married couple to get a divorce because I know that every marriage and/or situation is different. But what I am saying is that if you seek God for wisdom, he will respond. I'm also stressing that it's better to know your mate before entering into any covenant relationship, but also get to know *you* before your *boo.* Never settle for anyone or any situation that is not good for you. Ok, I'm done with that for now.

How It All Began

My husband and I got married after knowing each other for only seven months. Yep, seven months. I was going through a divorce at the time and had recently left my church of 25 years. I was all the way messed up and desperately trying to hold it together. My sister, best friend and I were sitting in the sanctuary of Word Assembly Church in Oakland, CA (shout-out to Bishop Keith L. Clark, he's awesome, by the way) when this minister, one that I'd never seen before that very day (my now husband, Julius Washington) was giving a sermonette on loving God, before the pastor spoke.

This man was wearing a plain white t-shirt and loose-fitting Girbaud jeans – why do I remember that specific thing when I can barely remember what I had for dinner the night before? My husband coined a term and would call this Herbnecia, for those with absent brains like mine. I have to call attention to what he was wearing because at the churches I've attended in the past, let's just say that this form of dress was completely unheard of. In the Baptist Church, it was unspokenly unacceptable for a preacher to be delivering the word – NO, *not* in the pulpit – wearing anything other than a suit. Let's just say I've never seen it before attending that ministry.

I remember whispering to my best friend and sister, "That's going to be my husband." Their reply was, "Girl, stop playing," as we laughed, and, of course, while he was still speaking, I responded, "For real, you'll see. That's going to be my husband." You see, in that moment I was absolutely positive that God spoke to me in a clear, still voice, informing me that we would marry, and the rest is literally history.

The way we started our relationship out was with consistent communication that eventually blossomed into an awesome relationship. We can literally talk about anything and everything, and that was evident from our first date on Jan. 1st, 2011, when we walked for several hours through an indoor mall, talking about almost everything in our pasts. For a person who didn't talk very much, with him, it would seem as if I had diarrhea of the mouth. I just felt that comfortable spilling all the tea. This partner of mine listens, some days better than others, and always gives me Godly advice. He is such a wonderful man and father, a great friend and powerful, effective lover – oh, did I say that? Yep, he's a keeper.

Now, the sex part (or shall I say, intercourse?) didn't actually happen until we were probably one year in. Yes you, heard me right, at least one year after we said, "I do." This was as a result of him having a prostatectomy that left him suffering from Erectile Dysfunction. According to Surgicaltech, "Prostatectomy as a medical term refers to the surgical removal of all or part of the prostate gland. This operation is done for benign conditions that cause urinary retention, as well as for prostate cancer and for other cancers of the pelvis."

Did I know this going in? Absolutely! You see, I fell in love with this delightful man, and the fact that he couldn't have a complete erection wasn't going to change my perspective or decision about loving him, and definitely not about marrying him. You see, when you place God where He needs to be, great things happen. All God expects from us is to trust, serve and leave the driving to Him. Now, keep reading for the good, gushy-gushy stuff.

Chapter 3 - *Communication*

Communication: Let's Talk About It!

Communication is key, and yes, it comes before love and trust because, without communication, it is not possible to discover love. Furthermore, love takes time, it grows, matures and, at some point, it peaks. At that stage, you know without a shadow of a doubt that God did His thang in hooking the two of you up. Isn't God amazing?

Communication is important to any relationship but absolutely imperative when it comes to a marriage. How can you communicate with your mate when the doorbell is broken, so to speak? Start at the beginning and don't leave anything out. Delve into who you really are, what your likes and dislikes are; this is essential to achieving a happy ending (I'm talking about sex) and more importantly, to building a lifelong successful team. The ending doesn't always mean an orgasm, although that would be great. Your objective should be satisfaction.

Let me help you: if you and your mate are making it do what it do and one of you climaxes after 5-10 minutes, who really wins or is satisfied? Now if your response was, "It's fine with me," you really need this book because after 5-10 minutes there shouldn't even be any insertion yet, but a lot of slobbering and licking going on.

The aim or goal in this regard is to be mentally and physically satisfied or to have a complete sense of fulfillment. My husband refers to a term, "safe sex talk" as being vital to any healthy sexual relationship. Safe sex talk in this context is defined as the freedom to explore and/or share with your partner their fantasies, positions and likes or dislikes about making love without the feelings of condemnation, shame or rejection. An example of this would be us sharing our views relating to sex without condemnation or negativity. "How can I tell this beautiful woman that I cannot achieve a complete erection any longer?" (We'll get to problems later) or "Is it safe to tell her that I, at times, would like to make love to her with her sexy underwear on?" An in-depth exploration is necessary and should include the feelings, needs, likes/dislikes, health concerns, limits, abilities etc. of each partner. This conversation should go far beyond the bedroom. And in the bedroom, communication should continue so that each person gets the most out of the experience.

In our bedroom we ask questions like, how does that feel? Do you like that? Are you okay? There should always be an ongoing dialogue to check in with each other at the various stages in the love-making process. This communication allows your partner to know that you care about their overall wellbeing and likewise gets you to the next stage or level in the relationship. And the goal here is to radiate when your partner is near. How many of you can actually say that you light up when your partner enters the room? And 5, 10 and even 20+ years down the road, will you still be able to take walks while holding hands, be able to be in each other's presence and just have fun, laugh because you are enthralled by each other's love?

And for goodness' sake, take your time; the process of love should never be rushed. Wait it out. Love will reach its peak in due time. Cooking often comes to mind when talking about this, and since this is no different, it reminds me of the steps in making beef short ribs – Oh, I love food that's done right! You can't just throw ribs into the pot with seasonings and expect them to be good. You have to prepare them, trim the fat, clean, season, flour and braise them.

Next, you need some cut onions and bell peppers to top them off and the final step is making that wonderful elixir called gravy. That's the preparation, next is the presentation. Jasmine rice and vegetables, and if you really want to show off, make some yams and corn bread. Ok, that was dinner last night. Anyway, the point to all of this is that there are steps and phases of love, and if the appropriate time is taken, the love will be amazing. My husband once told me that I overshare, but oh, I'm not quite done.

I remember when my husband told me about the difficulty he had in achieving a complete erection. My response at that time was, "It's ok." I remember the love felt and shown from him every day, and this was without intercourse; I had never felt that way before, never, nope, not ever.

The first time I'd gone to his apartment was on our second date. He cooked dinner for me. I was so impressed that he could cook, and when he asked me if I liked oxtails – we know what that answer was. He served oxtails, freshly prepared greens, and white rice, which he bought from a Chinese restaurant, so he wouldn't mess it up. The greens were killer, meaning damn good (my husband's greens are literally the best I've ever tasted), but the oxtails, well let's just say that the oxtails had a taste I'd never tasted before.

Well, they weren't bad but...frankly speaking, they weren't that great either. I'm used to them being prepared differently, like I cook them, so I guess I was just shocked is all. Gently, I asked, "What did you put in the oxtails?" He replied, "Red wine." Hmmm, that was it, the taste I had not yet experienced before, especially in the preparation of oxtails. "Are they ok?" he asked. "...yeah... They're ok," I replied. Let's just say, he's never cooked oxtails since. We leave the cooking up to me. Now barbeque? Yes, sir! That is his thing, and I don't tamper with the grill. I definitely know my lane; he can cook anything on the grill – simply amazing. I'm on a tangent now. As you can probably tell, I love to eat. However, the point of all this is to remind you to simply state or clearly communicate everything to your mate; even things that may appear small should be communicated. The more you know, the better together you will grow.

After dinner, we had a kiss-a-thon (that's what we coined it, anyway) as we looked back at our amazing first date.. The time seemed to run by like a stream of water. When we finally looked at the time, we were amazed to see that 6 hours had flown right by. And my hair, well, let me just say that it was cute before I got there, but a frizzy mess after our lips collided!

Wow! It reminds me of the song "I Like the Way (The Kissing Game)" by Hi Five. My husband definitely keeps me looking forward to another day, and I can truly say that I love the way(s) he makes me feel. Where had the time gone? We were enjoying each other's company, maybe a bit too much for a second date; we literally kissed half the night away and touched some, too, it was simply marvelous.

We did try later, although not that night, to have intercourse, but God said, "Nope, not happening!"

We were in Naples, Florida: a beautiful time, just him and me, and I remember him being so frustrated, but not me. I did care but wasn't bothered by not being able to fully have my husband the way we both imagined. I mean, I loved him so much already and believed that it really didn't make a difference because he gave me such satisfaction without plunging the apex.

I know you're probably thinking, how? Well, first, I was positive that God had told me that he was going to be my husband, so there was no wavering there. He was hand-delivered. Next, he was already a father and was wonderful with my two small children at the time (ages one and two). Moreover, he was tender with his words and his hands, but not in a sexual way, and that made me feel incredible.

To take it a step further, this man was always encouraging me and showered me daily with compliments (all new to me), all the while helping me understand God on a completely different level, and now that's what tipped the scale in his favor, but God knew it already – Go, Jesus! I must admit that this made me uncomfortable at first because I wasn't used to a man putting me first.

I mean he opened doors for me (waiting with the door open, and you know how we can be at times, ladies – or shall I say, like my momma, Slow!). Opening my door was a challenge for him for sure because many times I just bolted out of the car because it wasn't the norm for me. On the other hand, there were times when I felt bad because it meant he was getting out of the car just to open the door and get back in on those occasions when I would forget something in the house or would run into a store just to pick up knickknacks. I felt as if I were turning a jack in the box and knew exactly when he would pop out.

In his frustration, he would occasionally say, "Babe, let me be a man, please." He didn't even want me to take out the garbage or carry anything heavy; my husband literally inserts himself so that I can be who God created me to be, his helper. I was Queen, and for more than a day. He held me with compassion, saw me for who I was: beautifully hand-made by God, a rare commodity and, oh, he made me sing even without his dipper. Oh yeah, he's a keeper, and I'm so glad God happened when He did because He saved me through this man who I now call my soulmate. Thank You, Jesus!

Ok, Really, Communication!

There are times in a relationship when communication just does not seem to work. The reasons are numerous, but a few common ones are lack of respect, not seeing eye to eye, not giving the relationship the needed time, lack of patience, trust issues, not speaking the same language or the inability to comprehend what each individual needs. A big one is individuals bringing past hurts that trample and smother the relationship because they've never taken the time to resolve the issue or figure out its root cause. Thinking of communication deficits and how people respond reminds me of a few passages from the book *Men Are from Mars, Women Are from Venus*, by John Gray. Here's a synopsis of chapter 5:

Speaking Different Languages

Men talk in literal terms for the purpose of relaying information and women speak with dramatic vocabulary to fully express and relate their feelings.

Men like to sort their thoughts out before communicating them and have the tendency to become distant and non-communicative as they ponder their concerns. At this time, a woman needs reassurance that her partner still rates her as worthy of being taken care of. Women like to sort their thoughts out in the process of communicating them and have the tendency to pour forth a litany of general grievances as they relate their concerns. At the same time, a man needs reassurance that his partner still rates him as worthy of taking care of things.

There are times when it seems as if we're on different planets, but in all instances, it's vital that we communicate effectively so that our basic needs are met and so that our connection remains intact and strong. For example, think about our cell phones. If they don't have Wi-Fi or if the network connection is weak, Houston, we have a problem. We've all been there when this happens; the connection often drops or is nonexistent. Well, the same is true of communication with our mate: if we're unable to transfer the necessary information from one person to the other, our connection fails, and this is what puts our relationship in jeopardy.

A lack of communication leads to a disruption in the relationship. This interruption causes frustration on both parts, which leads to isolation, separation and, ultimately, if not repaired, can lead to divorce. This lack of communication can cause a negative perspective in one or both partners, a change in tone and behavior, conflicts or arguments, a lack of intimacy and loneliness.

Over time, if this flaw in communication continues, it can literally change the dynamic of the entire household, trickling down to our kids, who are sponges and thus learn this poor and non-effective communication language. Moreover, communication can be non-verbal, and most of us do it but may not even understand the impact on the other person.

What Does Nonverbal Communication Look Like?

Facial Expressions: According to EnkiVerywell and The Thought Catalog, there are at least 21 different facial expressions, but here are some common ones we tend to make on a regular basis: angry, happy, bored, confused, fear, excited and even that of being in love.

Eye Contact: The way we look at a person with a gaze or stare can indicate interest, hostility or even attraction. And the opposite is true, too: not looking or looking away during conversation could possibly indicate a person's deception. What are they thinking? It can also mean the person is thinking or trying to recall something said or that's on their mind. Not looking into the eyes of the person you're talking to could possibly mean that you are bored or that you're not interested in what's being said. Direct eye contact is very important, but, in some cultures, it can be a sign of disrespect, so it's valuable to know who you're dealing with.

Body Movement: Our body language can tell us a lot about ourselves and how we feel. For instance, crossing your hands during conversation can be interpreted as defensive, while slumping can suggest being lazy, disrespectful or disinterested. It's crazy when you think of the human body and how simple movements or adjustments can speak volumes. To ensure that you're not sending mixed signals, during conversations with your mate, try to keep your body elongated and faced towards them. This is telling them that you're interested in what they have to say.

Our bodies are constantly communicating, even if we're not aware of it. If during a conversation you turn away, cross your arms, start fidgeting or playing with your cell phone (or another object) or even start excessively yawning, etc., these actions could be possible signs letting them know you are not into what they're saying or perhaps it may not be the right time to talk. So just be aware when communicating that your body is not saying something completely different than what you intend.

Gestures: This includes waving our hands, pointing and using our fingers. Hand gestures, in my opinion, are like using an exclamation point to show how excited we are. They add emphases to what you're saying and can show your partner that you're totally into what they are saying, but the downfall is that, depending on the tone of the conversation, hand gestures can intensify the moment and may appear threatening to the receiver.

Touch: Oh, my favorite! Touch shows affection, love, sympathy, support, and concern for the other person. From a nurse's perspective, the element of touch is vital to human development. From holding hands while walking to a gentle massage before bed, it is important that we express our love for one another with this form of communication and not just in words alone. Touch relaxes the nerves and puts you into a different state of mind, also deemed necessary for mental and emotional stimulation.

Touch has been shown to affect both partners as it brings down the heart rate, soothing and relaxing the mind and body. Just think of how you feel after you make love and how relaxed you are. Interestingly, in an article in Psychology Today, Peter Anderson of San Diego University notes that atheists and agnostics touch more than religious individuals, "probably because religions often teach that some kinds of touch are inappropriate or sinful." Whew!

Interesting! I can see this because, in my religious experience, some teachers of the law get it wrong when it comes to God's word, why Jesus came or the idea that religion is what brings us closer to God. When it's really about a relationship with Him. Religion is controversial, yes, but so is the Bible. God welcomes touch and sex, and a lot of it (with your spouse), so touch would be a natural, loving way to stimulate your partner's whole mind and body.

Chapter 4 – What Is Love

LOVE

Love is patient, love is kind. It does not envy, it does not boast, it is not proud. It does not dishonor others, it is not self-seeking, it is not easily angered, it keeps no record of wrongs. Love does not delight in evil but rejoices with the truth. It always protects, always trusts, always hopes, always perseveres, 1 Corinthians 13:4-7 NIV

Oxford Dictionary defines love as "a profound tender affection, a feeling of deep personal attachment or affection as for a parent, child, or friend." Love is giving of yourself, a tenderness or deep devotion. Sure, there are many summations of the word love, but what does it mean to you? We often say, "I love you," but some are never taught what that simple phrase means. According to Thought Catalog, there are seven different types of love that originated in the Greek language: Eros, Philia, Agape, Storage, Ludus, Pragma and Philautia, but we will only cover four: Philautia, Agape, Eros and Pragma.

When I first met my husband, I met and quickly fell in love with a person who was confident in who he was, who loved God and in turn loved himself in the purest form. I, at that time in my life, was treading on a slippery slope. On the outside, I looked pretty good, but inside I was hurting, starved for affection and not knowing how to find my true self. But, God! God sent this man into my life to show me what true love was. It was a process, but I learned through my healing that there was no way for me to truly love anyone without first loving myself. Which brings me to our first kind of love, Philautia.

Philautia is the love for oneself. This kind of love has two components, a narcissistic kind of love where a person's first priority is self. Philautia is a selfish kind of love that leads to destruction, and this kind of love is unhealthy to oneself and in relationships. The other kind of Philautia represents a sincere love of self that is healthy, pure and unforced. This kind of love makes me think of the scripture given above (1 Corinthians 13:4-7). At the same time, this love is thought of as brotherly love, the platonic love of a friend. If we think about the relationship between a man and a woman, husband and wife, the two individuals that have developed the skill of loving oneself can have a dynamic relationship, deeply loving each other.

Agape is the closest love you can get to unconditional love. God demonstrated this love at the cross for mankind, a selfless kind of love. If we take this type of love and plug it into a relationship, we have love that does not keep score or need recognition. This love demonstrates giving of oneself without wanting anything in return.

To keep it real, this is also the kind of love that gives and gives and at times yields deficits in return. If you are giving with the wrong intentions, this love will leave you bitter. In other words, don't give to be seen or heard, or because you're expecting a pat on the back. Give because it's the right thing to do. In a healthy relationship, there will be times when you give 60, 70 or even 100% on any given day and get a minuscule amount in return. On the other hand, there will be days when this percentage is reversed, and eventually, this love will balance out. This kind of love doesn't keep score but keeps on giving.

Eros: If anyone can attest to passionately loving their mate and having it play over and again in their mind the next day, that's Eros. It is the passionate care, physical/sensual intimacy and affection demonstrated and received by your partner. According to learnreligions.com, "Eros is described as a romantic or sexual love. The term erotic is derived from eros." According to Christianity.com, "Eros is the word often used to express sexual love or the feeling of arousal that are shared between people who are physically attracted to one another. Eros is used in the Old Testament to express the physical and sensual intimacy between a husband and a wife..." I think this is self-explanatory.

Pragma is the last definition for this discussion. In this kind of love, the pragmatic lovers are founded on a basis of reason or duty. This love is said to be a longstanding love between couples that have been married for some time; this love develops as the years progress. In this type of love, sexual interests or desires take a back seat to compatibility, common goals, religion, politics, likes and dislikes. In my opinion, if you allow God to lead you in your relationship and work as a team, then the Pragma love theory is the one that God assigns. So, my personal definition when it comes to Pragma would be the demonstrated love in a relationship when you are led by God, so they are no longer two, but one flesh.

Therefore, what God has joined together, let no one separate. Matthew 19:6. The foundation of any great relationship begins with God, followed by compassion and love. Sex is so much more when you're faced with the man or woman you're crazy in love with. It branches out to be more than a feeling but a state of being, a way of living and a life with zeal and laughter.

What's Your Love Language?

I've heard my husband counsel many couples through the years and also comment on our relationship, telling folks, "I know her love language," and that it's important for them to know each other's love language. Well, what does this really mean? Over the years, I have understood it to mean how you want to receive love from your partner or how you want to be loved. Let's see if you can answer this: Ask yourself if you know what your partner's view on love is and/or what love means to them.

My husband often refers to this book he read years ago, and I've found in this research that the author, Dr. Gary Chapman, after counseling numerous couples, came up with a way for people to express their emotions and love through five categories or languages of love. The name makes perfect sense: The Five Love Languages. I've never actually read the book, but my husband speaks of it often. The five love languages are words of affirmation, quality time, receiving gifts, acts of service and physical touch.

Without even knowing what these entail, you may already know what your view of love is and how you want to be shown love. The question is, have you ever expressed this to your partner? If not, how will they ever know, for example, that you like to be hugged every day, and that a hug is how you internalize the love felt by them.

For me, I don't think I've ever really communicated it in this way, but my husband pays close attention to what I like or the look on my face, not to mention the comments I make after he's given me something. He knows that I love flowers, and not just on Mother's Day or my birthday. Giving me flowers just because means that he has gone out of his way to do something special for me. Now, buying flowers may not be a big deal to some, but it shows that he's thinking of me and what will make my day better. He actually calls these things "Cha-Ching."

A Cha-Ching or deposit is when you do something exceptional, and the other person isn't expecting it; it's a signal of love and an outward form of expression. And the opposite, a deficit is when a person continues to make withdrawals from the love account, putting the relationship in jeopardy. As for my husband, he loves to be catered to. He wouldn't actually put it that way, but he loves when I cook wonderful meals and make his plate. He also loves when we spend quality time together. It can just be watching a television program together.

My husband is spoiled, but then again, so am I. We both love time spent together, and both of us need words of affirmation and telling each other throughout the day that we love each other. So, if you don't know what your spouse needs from you, ask but also observe, and step outside of the box to be creative; it will always work in your favor.

What Do They Need or Want From Me?

This is a big one. Most couples never take the time to ask this simple question. I had to ask myself what I needed from my now-husband when we were dating, when he came right out and told me what he needed from me. He also told me what he was capable of versus not. I didn't know it then, but he was setting himself up for a wonderful position of power and control. By way of definition, power and/or control is the ability to direct or influence the behaviors of others or their course of events.

You see, when I first saw him and heard him speak, what rang true was his love for God and the deep love he had for his family. Now, when I actually met him, I was able to see his compassionate side and felt the love and concern he had for those around him. He was a man that was kind, gentle and knew his worth, and that was so sexy to me. I know this may seem weird, but I've told him several times that it's a huge turn-on for me the way he loves the Lord and is committed to HIM. Jackpot!!

My husband demonstrates this love every day, thereby teaching me and our eight kids how to love. He loves God and is a stickler for truth, thereby teaching us to know God for ourselves, to read and study the word and develop a relationship with Him for ourselves. And boy oh boy, is he adamant about not following others but developing your own unique individualism, and he tells everyone to never get tired of doing what's right, Galatians 6:9. My husband has incredible power and leads his family the way God directs him – he's amazing, told ya!

Ok, so back to the needs: my husband made sure to tell me of his needs early on and also informed me of his capacity so that, in my opinion, I wasn't going to ask him for something years down the line that he wasn't going to be able to fulfill. *Brilliant!* I said all of that to say how valuable it is to set yourselves up for success and communicate one another's needs. Perhaps you'll find that in doing so, it will clear many things up and help your partner know you on a different level.

At the same time, when the lists are exchanged, one may find that they're not able to handle or accommodate something on the list. Now, just because something on the list doesn't appear to be attainable or realized, doesn't mean that you should run to the courthouse and file for divorce. Absolutely not! It just means that there needs to be compromise. Set expectations, thereby letting the other person know what not to expect from you.

I remember a couple of years later, our then pastor, Bishop Keith Clark, did a sermon on needs vs. wants that put things into perspective for me. This was my take-away: he informed the congregation that a NEED was something (a person, place, or practice) that was necessary for the empowerment, the enrichment, and the development of your life. He defined a need as being something you could not live without, something that was crucial to your being. Bishop Clark then went on to instruct us to write our own list, making two columns, one being needs and the other being wants.

Now came the crucial part, when we had to ask ourselves whether that thing we listed was necessary for our empowerment, our enrichment, or our development, and if it wasn't, well then it was clearly a want. This is actually a great tool for everyone, especially for those in relationships, because it will help redefine who you are and what you need in the relationship or marriage so that the union can be successful. So, I advise any person reading this book to compose their own list. Once the list is complete, share it with your partner to help them fully understand you and realistically meet your needs. Perhaps if you look at your relationship as a love game, you can use the needs as a set of rules that will help guide the other player, giving him or her a playing advantage to be successful.

Why I Love Him

At some point, you need to ask yourself what you love about your partner. I mean you do, right? Can you sort out your emotions and put them into actual words? The point of this journey is asserting yourself and holding onto the love that God has for you, exploring and laying the fundamental groundwork so that you can have amazing intimacy between the two of you. I would say the goal of ascertaining the "why" is loving your mate with everything you have and not holding anything back.

Can you deny yourself, or perhaps remove yourself and any issues you may be harboring, not to mention the drama that comes along with these issues, that prevents you from loving your partner? *You, you, you* – it comes back to *you* in exploring why you love your partner. What perhaps does the love he or she delivers do for or add to you? Are you able to isolate that love and still be made whole? If not, well then it is then time for self-discovery and perhaps looking in the mirror to see who you are and what you, yourself bring to the table. You see, in loving any person, you must first love **you**.

Why I love my husband is because he adds to me. He completes me in a way that is almost indescribable, and that makes me feel as if I'm unstoppable, we're unstoppable. My husband helps me find my center when I'm at my wits' end and when I feel like I can't make it. He aligns the fragments that have been pulled apart during the struggle of our day-to-day lives.

I love him because God handed him over to me when I was lost and in despair. I love him because I know the value of the gift God gave me, and I hold it dear to my heart, trying every day to be better. I love him because I know that life is but a vapor; as James 4:14 says, we're here today and gone tomorrow, and I don't dare waste this precious time we have. If you can't put your love into words, **try** because it will help you see what you have and hopefully you will treat it with value and discover the gem that is placed right in front of you.

Chapter 5 – *Health and Maintenance*

Our Health Challenges

When I got to this section of the book, I chuckled because of what I was going to include, confidently knowing that God intended it to help many people in our situation. I'll start with myself. At age 17, I was diagnosed with rheumatoid arthritis (a chronic autoimmune inflammatory disorder that attacks healthy joints and causes pain, stiffness and swelling).

At that time, I had horrible pain in my right hip and missed a lot of school, and I vividly remember walking across the graduation stage with crutches because I couldn't walk independently. Over the years, I learned how to manage my pain and lived a pretty productive life, but unfortunately, about 10 years later, I was diagnosed with osteoarthritis (a disorder in which the protective cartilage that cushions the ends of your bones wears down, therefore causing pain, stiffness, swelling and loss of flexibility). Lucky me.

Approximately 15 years later, I came down with something that changed the course of my life, causing me to lose my job and reducing my quality of life: chronic fatigue syndrome. This disease is much harder to diagnose, and I spent the next two years in agony while the doctors tried to figure it out, giving it a name. Chronic fatigue is characterized by extreme fatigue that can't be explained by an underlying medical condition. I was incredibly weak and at times not even able to get to the toilet by myself.

The pain I thought was already bad from the arthritis was magnified with this disorder, and at times every joint in my body hurt. This disease also brought on frequent migraines, and I suffered an average of five days per week, every week, going back and forth to the emergency room and MD office (until they finally prescribed a treatment that worked).

My sleep was a thing of the past, interrupted every night, and on a good night, I was able to get three hours uninterrupted. Oh, but no need to stop there. I had a sore throat and cold symptoms all the time, I had involuntary muscle twitches and seemed to have a hard time concentrating and remembering things.

Life was bad, but then there was God! I truly had to learn a few things, and one of them was trusting Him. Regardless of how devastating my situation or view of things was, He allowed me to live the scripture: **God will supply all of your needs**, Philippians 4:19. At the same time, I had to remember Proverbs 3:5 NIV, **Trust in the Lord with all your heart and lean not to your own understanding, in all your ways acknowledge Him and He will make your paths straight.**

You see, at that time, I went from bringing in $95K a year to receiving food stamps. My husband was still working as a truck driver but two years later retired early because of a work injury that almost cost him his life. Come on now, for those of you who are believers, you should be shouting with me right now. *God is a Way-Maker!*

So, how did we survive? Well, my husband was able to get unemployment of $1600 per month, and God did the rest. For those non-believers, it started with a money order (from an anonymous sender) that was put in our mailbox that said,

"God loves you and so do I" for $1500. Months down the line, a couple told us that the Holy Spirit told them to give us a love offering on a regular basis, and this went on for the next two years. (Thank you for being obedient, you know who you are.) My parents and family rallied around us, filling in the gaps with love, food and parenting our then, four and five-year-olds. My sister even lowered our rent. Are you shouting with me yet? God is so amazing and is worthy of being praised.

You see, at that time, I was crying more times than not because of my failing health that the doctors couldn't cure, but I had peaks of praise that over time allowed me to move out of a state of depression and into a state of thankfulness.

I know you think the story's over, but after I was diagnosed with chronic fatigue, I was later diagnosed with atrial fibrillation (irregular heartbeat or fast rhythm) after a few nights' stay in the hospital when my heart just would not behave. I couldn't catch my breath, and it felt as if my heart wanted to bounce right out of my chest. I went on medication intermittently to control the rhythm but stopped when my blood pressure got so scarcely low, I honestly believed I wouldn't make it.

My latest diagnosis is fibromyalgia. Funny story, my father, who is now home with the Lord, told me one day over the phone that he had fibromyalgia. I said, "What!" He replied, "Yes, I have fibromyalgia." "Dad, when did the doctor give you that diagnosis?" He already suffered from heart disease and issues with his spine that rendered him in horrible pain. His reply was, "I got it off the television." I laugh now because he had his own set of medical challenges, and fibromyalgia wasn't one of them, at least, not officially. But after his death was when I was diagnosed with it.

With my fibromyalgia (widespread muscle pain accompanied by fatigue, impaired sleep, memory, and mood issues) diagnosis in 2018, I've already had hip replacement surgery and multiple injections and procedures trying to relieve the pain, but nothing thus far has made a significant difference. The widespread pain to various parts of my body can be more than overwhelming because medication at times isn't effective. Each day is a challenge for sure, but I have to count it all a joy if I wake up at all.

You see, even though it's hard most days, I can now look at life as a blessing and not a curse, not dwelling on my situation because situations are known to change, right?

Philippians 4:8 MSG, **Summing it all up, friends, I'd say you'll do best by filling your minds and meditating on things true, noble, reputable, authentic, compelling, gracious — the best, not the worst; the beautiful, not the ugly; things to praise, not things to curse.** This scripture is one that will bless your soul, and if you're depressed, it will help you see what truly matters in life.

I've learned to stop focusing on my condition and start focusing on what was in front of me: my husband, children, mother, and my siblings. Focusing on them made me smile; they even made me realize that I had something to live for. Moreover, I learned to start praising and thanking God for the things I had. **If you stop and take the time to praise God long enough, the negative things in your life will start to take on a different look.** Those things that you deemed horrendous will start to look smaller, harmless, and less important. Praising God allowed me to see Him in a different light.

During my downtime, I learned to look up and see who was in charge: GOD! I developed a relationship with the

Master, and that's honestly what changed my focus. It was like a ship being steered by the captain, you don't always feel the direction, the motion, the undercurrents or even the turn of the wheel, but soon you come to realize that you're in a different place, a completely different location in life. Praise God now and see how your life will change.

As for my husband, well, he's a walking miracle if I do say so myself. My husband was diagnosed with prostate cancer in 2009. He then underwent the surgical procedure to remove the prostate gland known as a laparoscopic prostatectomy. The surgery was a success, and to this day my husband remains cancer free, praise God! However, one year later, to the date, he received news after a regular optical exam that he had a mass on his brain that needed to be removed. WOW, God, really! This also happened to be the time we spoke on the phone for the first time, the day (December 28th, 2010) I decided to give him a call.

Him being a Minister didn't stop his feelings of overwhelming pending doom because, after all, he is just a man with human feelings, like any other man, but I'll say it again, "But God!" He was told by his pastor at the time, Bishop Clark, "What God did before, he reserves the right to do again," and, well, God certainly turned the tables. My husband is a strong testament to those around him, and he tells people whenever he gets the chance of his testimony to encourage them. In my opinion, that's what God really wants from all of us, **Praise**.

It's just like the 10 leapers that Jesus healed: Luke 12:11-19, and only one of them came back to say, "Thank you" (Jesus' response was, "Where are the other nine? Didn't anyone else return to give praise to God?").

You see, it really doesn't matter what we go through, what counts is our ability to praise God for what he's done. And as for my husband's tumor, the surgery removed most of the mass that was pressing on his optic nerve, thereby obscuring his vision. He also had a series of radiation treatments to shrink the tumor cells that were left.

Today, thankfully, the mass still remains the same size, small and not a bother (10 years later). The effects of the brain mass, coupled with treatments, left him with hormonal imbalances, and he started exhibiting symptoms of weight loss, fatigue, altered mood and feeling sick all the time. The problem was found to be a lack of the production of testosterone and cortisol (essential hormones). And now he takes a replacement hormone for the cortisol, and I give him bi-monthly testosterone injections to keep his levels normal.

As if these things weren't enough, he had a work injury in which a box hit him over the head, which forced him into early retirement, a sure blessing that he is meant to be alive. I remember him coming home that evening, his left leg dragging, and favoring his left arm. I immediately thought he'd had a stroke and did a quick assessment, but things didn't add up. Still, I knew he needed medical attention. I stressed the importance and the urgency for him to be seen, but of course, he refused!

Why on earth are men so darn stubborn? This was Friday evening, and all I could do was pray. Saturday was much the same. His symptoms didn't get worse, but they didn't get any better either. But Sunday morning was on the horizon.

Sunday, we went to a visiting church and the ministers asked him to join them on the pulpit. As he walked up the only three stairs, he struggled, and it was obvious to everyone that he didn't have good muscle control on his left side. I urged the family to pray and to talk to him about going to the hospital, but no luck there. As we sat at brunch (yes, we went to eat), my parents talked to him and thankfully, he finally agreed to go to the hospital.

When we got to the emergency room, they immediately admitted him and after taking diagnostic tests, they found that he was bleeding on the brain (a subdural hematoma). They told him that he was lucky he came in when he did because he could have died. Remember, this was Sunday – Resurrection Day, if you ask me. The triage nurse asked him, "Do you know the number one killer or cause of deaths in men?" His response was, "Hypertension?" "No", she said. "Heart Disease?" was his second response. The nurse responded, "No, it's stubbornness."

Now if you're a believer, you know it was only God that kept him. They quickly transferred him to another hospital, where we were met by a surgeon who informed us that he was going to have a craniotomy early the next morning. As I said early on, my husband is a walking miracle.

Here's my point: everybody will have some health challenges during the course of their lives, some more than others. If you have strong faith and a healthy support system, whether that support is family, friends, or congregational support, whatever it is for you, you *can* get through it. There is a song called "Keep the Faith" by Charles Jenkins that speaks to this. Check it out, it's a good one. All points lead to God. He will always be there to see you through.

Making Love with Health Challenges

I'm so thankful that I have my husband by my side. I told you before, he's a keeper. When individuals have health challenges, making love takes a back seat, and this may leave some people with feelings of frustration at the very least. Although we have empathy for our mates, the fact remains that we still have needs.

This section deals with *our* health challenges and how *we* overcame them. It's important to note that whatever the health challenge, you can get through it, together. Both partners need to be included in the plan so that both will find fulfillment.

As for us, our physical challenges came in the form of pain, fatigue, erectile dysfunction, and depression. It is important to note depression because having any disability or problem that affects the human body for an extended period of time affects the brain. At the same time, certain medications that you take can have an adverse effect on the body, and sex again becomes either a thing of the past or becomes more challenging to accomplish.

Since I aired our dirty laundry earlier, I'll start with me. I have a slew of challenges with my body, it's true. But if I had to list just two things that give me the most difficulty, they would be horrible pain and extreme fatigue. I've had pain so long that I, for the most part, have learned how to manage it and go about my day. There are days, though, that the pain stops me in my tracks, and I can't seem to function. Even the simplest task like getting out of bed can be problematic on bad days, and my husband eagerly assist me, and this is with pain medication.

It's days like these that mark another day without love-making, and although my husband is completely understanding and wouldn't dare dream of suggesting sex, it's frustrating on my part, and at times makes me feel less of a woman not to be able to perform. When you have feelings like these, it is important that you pray, meditate, and find solace in the Lord. Otherwise, insanity, depression and negativity will linger and can create a wedge between you and your partner.

Let him or her in; tell them what's going on and how you're feeling, and never internalize or keep anything to yourself. Sharing or communicating your thoughts increases awareness. It keeps you on the same page and allows the bond between you to become stronger than ever. Here are a couple of scriptures that you can use to keep you mentally strong:

Isaiah 40:29 NIV, **He gives strength to the weary and increases the power of the weak.**

2 Corinthians 12:9 NIRV, **But he said to me, "My grace is all you need. My power is strongest when you are weak." So, I am very happy to brag about how weak I am. Then Christ's power can rest on me.**

It is my experience that when you're mentally weak, it can lead to mental overload and then depression. It is there that you start to isolate yourself and speak negatively. You have to say, "Nope, not today!" Empower yourself so that you can get to a place of mental strength. Moreover, when one of you is weak in the relationship and feeling low, it is there that the other should step in with some form of encouragement and demonstrate love and compassion, knowing that the other partner may not be able to encourage him or herself.

Pain and How We Get Through It to Get to It

This section deals with learning ways to manage your pain and improve your health so that you can have a fantabulous and passionate love-making experience.

Seek Medical Attention

First, it is important that you seek medical attention and find out where your pain is stemming from so that you don't further aggravate your symptoms and cause more damage to that site. As a retired nurse, it's my experience that some individuals don't trust doctors and therefore don't seek medical attention or advice, keeping them locked in their pain and suffering.

And then there are those who want the help because their pain is too intense but don't actually follow the plans of care outlined by a medical professional. I've actually been there and lived the latter experience. I've heard it said that nurses are horrible patients, and I guess it's true.

I hate the excruciating pain that I'm in more often than not, but I also hate the side effects of my medication and how it makes me feel at times. There have been times that I try to endure the pain and see if it will either taper off or just go away so that I don't have to take my prescribed medicine. The problem with that is, if I wait too long to take the medication, the intensity of the pain increases and the medication that I should have taken hours before is no longer effective in managing my pain, thereby leaving me in agony.

Typing these words, I realize I sound like a crazy person. If you suffer from pain, the very best advice I can give you is to stay ahead of the pain by following the plan of care outlined by your doctor and taking the prescribed medication on a regular basis for control. Yes, I'm well aware of the damage that pain medication can have on your organs over time, but I also know that living with pain – being in pain without a means of control – is pure insanity.

They do have newer medication on the market that targets arthritic pain; however, for me, I choose not to take these because some of them block your tumor necrosis factor. And since my family has higher incidences of cancer, I don't want to increase the likelihood of me getting it, so I opt out. You have to pick your poisons in life, weigh your options and see what treatment(s) are best for you. Don't, for any reason, let yourself be forced into a treatment plan or medication that you aren't comfortable with, so do your research before.

I have tried what seems to be every over-the-counter cream and spray that claims to combat pain. I start with these first to see how effective they will be. I like Bio-Freeze, Stop Pain, and something I've tried recently, Mary's Medicinal rub, the best. Trust me, I don't have stock in these items and am not getting a dime to say this, but they work the best in managing certain types of pain, or at least taking the edge off.

In my experience, what you use to control the pain depends on the origin. If the pain is topical or stemming from the muscle, the creams or sprays work better. It's that darn joint and spinal pain that drives me crazy and is the hardest to control. In addition to the over the counter and narcotic medications, I've also tried both THC and CBD (internally) for control but in the end stopped using them because the CBD pills didn't touch my spinal pain (works better for muscle strains) and the THC made me high, and I didn't like that feeling.

I do, however, recommend anyone to try these options because they have been known to be beneficial for pain control, but be wise and discuss it with your doctor first because they can have harmful effects on the body (with certain medical conditions). My husband was a believer when he had cranial surgery that left him with nagging headaches and sometimes migraines that Tylenol, Motrin, or the prescribed medication couldn't touch. He actually used THC for these symptoms, and it totally worked in managing his pain. It didn't take the headache away completely, but it did reduce it by approximately 75%. ⌬ And when not using opioids, I had no constipation, which is one of the common side-effects of their use.

Another method for pain control that I currently use is the TENS unit. This small device (with electrode pads) works by sending electrical currents to the surface of the skin and nerves. The impulses work by encouraging endorphins (our natural pain killers), thereby relieving or reducing pain felt. The stimulation feels as if it has massage-like components that soothe tired muscles, and it is of great benefit when it comes to pain relief.

If you're suffering from pain and have tried it "your way" for some time now and that doesn't seem to be working, go to the doctor! If you've tried the care plans that your doctor has outlined and that hasn't worked either, go back and communicate the effectiveness of the plan, and advocate for yourself so that he or she can come up with a new one that you are more comfortable with. And if you are not comfortable speaking up for yourself, take a family member or friend along to be your mouthpiece.

Quite frankly, if your doctor is not working for you or meeting your needs, transfer to another one. There's always more than one cook in the kitchen. And if that's not the case, then you probably know someone who has a great doctor. Send out the smoke signals until you find the right MD. If your diagnosis or health history is complex like mine, then at the very least you need a physician who listens. What's the bottom line? If you've tried what seems to be **everything**, try something else. Be diligent in the search until you find the right apple in the bunch. Isn't your health and care worth it?

Physical Therapy - Depending on your diagnosis it may be beneficial to seek out or ask for a referral to physical therapy. If you've tried therapy before and it didn't seem to help, is it that you stopped the plan of care outlined for you, or perhaps that you didn't see it through till the end? The goal of therapy is to aid in physical mobility and independence, and these plans must be carried out for the long haul – that is if you want a favorable outcome. If you've been in pain for some time and have not seen a physical therapist before, what's the holdup? It's time to take charge of your own health and not leave it solely in the doctors' hands. If you don't take charge, who will?

On the other hand, if you've exhausted the P.T. option and found it not to be effective in managing your pain, what's imperative is that you find another mechanism or way of controlling it. To the best of your ability, stay healthy, strong, and flexible. Not for the goal of sex in mind but for your own vitality; but then again, whatever gets you moving and motivated, do that. Remaining in good physical health when you have a history of pain enables the muscles in the body to perform at their best. So, at your own comfort level, get off the couch and find an activity that works best for you. Whether it is:

- Walking or taking a hike
- Swimming (best form of exercise without injuring joints. It works everything, so, if you can, do!)
- Bike riding (a stationary bike will do just fine)
- Yoga (there are different variations of yoga; I've tried those pertaining to arthritis)

Do what works best for your body, and try not to be intimidated by social media, television or keeping up with the Joneses. If you're a novice, start out by performing at least 20 minutes of consistent activity each day (for cardiovascular health) – more if this is not your first rodeo, so to speak. And just a side note when it comes to endurance in the bedroom, nothings is worse than conking out when you've just gotten started, so work up to a good regime that keeps you in the best physical health possible. Make it a way of life.

Food for thought: heart disease doesn't begin when the doctor first gives you the diagnosis. It actually starts years before, so be good to your body, and it will in turn be good to you in the years to come. Eat right, exercise and get into a good mental space or the right frame of mind.

Medication – Whatever the doctor prescribes, take it (look it up first to see if it interferes with any other medication you may be taking; not all doctors check this. Drugs.com is a great website for this). You can also experiment with over-the-counter medications like Tylenol or Motrin (or Ibuprofen) to see if they're effective for pain control. Read your labels and don't consume more than the daily recommended dosage as it can be toxic to your kidneys and liver. Also, check with your doctor to see if any of these OTC medications are contraindicated with your current medications.

Prayer/Meditation – Take the time to meditate and/or talk to your Heavenly Father. This is not a time to perseverate or worry about fears or concerns, but a time to give all of your troubles and cares to the one who is able to handle them, the problem solver. Consider it a necessary time-out to keep you centered. Find a quiet place, just you, and try to blot out any distracting thoughts that may enter your mind. Practice slow, deep rhythmic breaths, as this will help release any tension you may have which subsequently may be adding to the stress that is causing your pain.

Ice vs. Heat – When you have pain, you will learn to try just about anything you can to reduce or get rid of it. At the same time, using things that won't damage your internal organs is always a win. Over the course of 34 years of dealing with pain, I've always hated applying ice to my body because I just hate being cold. But now that I'm having my own personal summer (all year long, I might add), I'm starting to see ice in a different light. Here's the deal regarding when to use ice and/or heat for pain control:

Ice – Ice works by blocking the pain receptors that cause pain. So, it's best to use ice at the onset of an injury to help reduce the swelling, and likewise, the pain. Also, if you have sciatica, using ice on the lower back can aid in relief. You can actually apply an ice pack for any element of pain; it starts out cold as hell but then it brings on a numbing effect that is really beneficial.

Heat – Heat works by stimulating blood circulation and relaxing the muscle. If you're dealing with chronic pain, stiffness or sore muscles, heat calms the storm so to speak. It assists in relaxing the nerves and muscles to relieve the pain.

It's important to note when using either ice or heat that you don't apply it directly to the skin as it can cause damage (blisters, swelling, changes in skin color, etc. If any of these occur, seek medical attention). Use a thin towel, pillowcase, or garment to wrap around the ice/heat pack and only apply it for increments of 15-20 minutes at a time, allowing your skin to return to a normal temperature before re-applying it. For example, try 15 minutes on, 15 minutes off and so on.

Herbs – If you are looking for more of a homeopathic approach to managing your pain, there are herbs out there that claim to work in assisting with relief. Again, depending on the origin of the pain, certain herbs work by decreasing the inflammation that causes pain. Do your research, experiment with various ones, and wait the allotted time (minimum of two weeks) to see if they work for you before giving up. What works for one person may not have the same effect for another. And always check with your doctor before implementing herbs or natural supplements as they can interact with certain medications, increasing or decreasing their effectiveness and possibly cause untoward effects in the body.

Here is a list of herbs that I found on Paindoctor.com that decrease inflammation and are good for pain relief:

- Oregano
- Cumin
- Rosemary
- Nettle
- Garlic

- Sage
- Turmeric (good relief)

There may be more, but these are a few common ones and some that I've actually incorporated myself. I like simmering the herbs and drinking them as a tea. In my experience, they seem to help with decreasing pain but also with relaxation. Each day you wake up is a new day to rediscover a new you. So, keep at it until you find the right concoction that works.

Foods and Maintaining Health

We've all heard at some point in our lives, and most of us know, that we should eat fresh over processed, but do we understand how foods can play a role in how we feel and operate? Growing up, food was always the central theme in our gatherings, so it's not unusual that I look at food as a hobby, a necessity, and, quite frankly, as a pick-me-up. My sister and I share a love of bread (among other things), fresh especially, and there were times when we would eat loads of it with just butter and/or mayonnaise. Now, you know the bread is good when you can eat it with mayonnaise – or do you?

And don't get me started on processed foods. They're great, but no one thinks of the damage that decades of eating too much of the wrong foods are inflicting on the body as we scarf them down. I've learned that you can still enjoy those goodies from time to time, but moderation is definitely key.

Food can literally change the dynamic of our internal bodies, and there is tons of literature to back that up, just not in this book. Sure, certain illnesses can stem from genetic conditions, side effects from the medicines we take, obesity, smoking or alcohol consumption. But our diets (what we put in our mouths – food, that is!) are the key to maintaining an overall healthy body and decreasing the inflammation that causes pain. "More importantly, the right food choices for a sustained amount of time can also reverse some of the damage done to our bodies over those past decades," says Glyn Poole of Train4Life Fit Co.

When my husband was diagnosed with prostate cancer, the doctor told him that his diet was most likely one of the culprits; go figure. He added that eating fresh berries, the intake of cruciferous vegetables and decreasing the amount of grilled meats were important in decreasing the likelihood of a recurrence. And due to a possible likelihood of genetic factors, his son should also follow these guidelines.

To jump back on the bandwagon of foods and health, below is a list of some conditions that eating a poor diet can contribute to over an extended period of time.

- High cholesterol
- Heart disease
- Stroke
- Type 2 diabetes
- High blood pressure
- Fatigue
- Inflammatory bowel disorder

- Constipation
- Pain
- Some forms of cancer

The big question is, why wait until you're inflicted with an illness or start exhibiting signs or symptoms that something has gone awry before taking charge of your health? Sad as it may seem, many individuals wait until they get that bad news before making the necessary adjustments to their health. But then, there are those like my father who found it extremely difficult to make a committed step to change and is, unfortunately, not with us today because of it.

My father loved his fried foods. And even though he had high cholesterol, high blood pressure, and clogged arteries, well, he just couldn't leave certain foods alone, although he tried on occasion. I remember talking to him and telling him that baked was better than fried, and his response was, "Dear, I just like my meat in a little grease."

What I've learned over the years, even though culturally, food was at the very core of it all, is that it is never too late to make changes in the way we look at food. For me, it was when both of my younger children were given the diagnosis of pre-cholesterol and pre-diabetes. Now, that was the catalyst that made me change a few things in our home.

At the same time, my own health was failing, and I needed to make a difference, if not for myself then for my innocent children. Please don't get me wrong, we still have our occasional treats and indulge in foods like ice cream, cookies and pizza, but it's not a daily or consistent occurrence. Moreover, when my father died of a heart attack in 2017, it was then tangible evidence for our family that what we put in our mouths affects the outcome of our bodies later in life.

Examples of some unhealthy foods (these should only be eaten in moderation):

- Pizza
- Fast food
- Fried foods
- Lunch meats*
- Hot dogs*
- Bacon*
- Doughnuts/pastries
- Cookies
- Candy
- Potato chips
- White bread
- White flour
- Sugar
- Soda/sugary drinks
- Alcohol in excess

*Processed foods that are cured with a high amount of salt and fat.

Now, when it comes to pain, specifically auto-immune disorders, foods that increase the inflammatory process in the body should be eaten in moderation or not at all, depending on the level of your pain, not to mention the disorder. What might be a good idea is to experiment and remove certain foods from your diet and keep a journal to document how you feel each day. If you're not sure if it's working, then one by one add the foods back into your diet and compare the symptoms. Foods that increase inflammation in the body are:

- Dairy
- Soy
- Gluten
- Nightshades: tomatoes, potatoes, eggplant and peppers
- Alcohol
- Sugar
- Processed foods: refined carbohydrates/boxed/shelved foods
- Foods high in omega-6: corn, cottonseed, vegetable oil blends, safflower
- Caffeine: chocolate, tea, soda and energy drinks
- Meat: red meat, processed meats
- Cheese (cheese is high in fat, so the serving size per day should be followed. At the same time, to reduce inflammation, limit intake altogether.)

Just to reiterate, if you have a high inflammation count, these are probably the culprits.

Getting back to unhealthy foods, if we eat these foods in moderation or not at all, our overall health and mental wellbeing will improve, not to mention the weight you're likely to shed – yippee!

Sometimes our lifestyle and finances can dictate the foods we eat. When you're on a fixed income or in a lower financial bracket, I know all too well that eating healthy can sometimes cost considerably more. At the same time, there may be days when you're tired from work and need to feed your family in a pinch, and what seems to fit in that moment is a drive-by to your local fast-food eatery to get the job done. I remember looking for the value meals and comparing fast-food sites for the best deal because I was just too tired to cook after work.

In retrospect, what I was doing was damaging our bodies and teaching our kids the poor habit of choosing the wrong foods that would be ingrained in them forever. I soon changed the breads to whole grains, stopped buying juice boxes and sodas, changed the snacks from cookies to goldfish and the frequency of eating fried foods and those high in fat to a seldom occurrence. Flipping the switch on them was hard, and to this day is sometimes a struggle, but I have to keep telling myself that I'm the adult, the one in charge, the sensei, so to speak, the dictator over our dietary practices.

A tip for parents: There's no reason for our kids to be unhealthy or even obese when we are the ones with the cash card, the ones with the car who walk the aisles of the grocery stores and then come home and prepare the meals. It starts with us; we're the ones who are leading by example, so let's power through it and make wise choices.

So, what's the takeaway? I'm glad you asked! Eating a healthier diet can be enjoyable and attainable if we'd only place a value on ourselves and those around us. I personally want my family to look and feel more vibrant. I want us to be energized, and most importantly, to be healthy and have a better quality of life.

The truth is, eating out, although convenient, will likely cost more in the long run as opposed to shopping for the right foods. But making the wise decision to focus on overall health and healthier food practices, like implementing fresh fruits and veggies, incorporating beans and healthy grains, and setting aside processed items can actually save money, and more importantly, lives. This practice and way of thinking just requires more thoughtfulness and intention. Remember, you've got this. Just make the decision to truly live.

What Can I Do?

Learn to plan your meals, write them down and incorporate the kids in the shopping experience, meal preparation and cooking. It will not only educate your family, but they will learn to adopt a better lifestyle in the future. Do it before they get too old because teens would much rather spend time on their electronics as opposed to helping in the kitchen. In other words, develop healthy practices while they're young.

And if you don't know where to begin, start with research. Next, do an inventory of your cabinets and refrigerator as to what you're feeding your family. Don't stop there but take it a step further and remove all the items that you know are working against your health; it's incredibly hard not to eat the cookies or chips if they're only "hidden away." How many of you have put the M&M's away or folded the chip bag down, telling yourself that you are not eating anymore, but soon find yourself opening that darn bag minutes later, saying, "Just a few more" and finding that they're all gone? **If you don't have it, you can't eat it!**

Next, visualize the foods you love to eat the most, write down what they are and see what nutritional value they have, if any. And please do talk to your doctor. See what your laboratory values say about your overall health and what you can do to correct them, if anything.

Don't stop there, but start the conversation with your MD or nutritionist for guidance on how to begin because it's often hard for people to take the initial first steps. Healthcare these days is geared towards preventive health maintenance and most plans cover nutritional visits for free. It's more cost-effective to teach a patient good health practices instead of managing an actual disease. And make sure you take advantage of all your pre-screening tests; they're there to help you maintain optimal health and let you know if there is anything looming in the body. Just know that you are the change your family needs, so why not begin now?

The following information is taken from The American Heart Association and Web MD, but again, discuss any changes in your dietary practices with your physician because everyone's health conditions vary, and some people may need a reduction or addition. (These numbers also vary based on height, weight, sex, age and activity level, according to Glyn Poole.)

- Daily Fat intake – 44-77%
- Daily Sugar – 6-9 tsp (a 12oz can of soda has 8tsp)
- Daily Carbs – 45-65%
- Daily Protein – 25-30 grams

Below is a chart that may help when shopping for the correct foods:

Healthy Eating List

Fruit	Vegetables	Dairy	Protien
Strawberries	Romaine	Greek	Chicken
Blueberries	lettuce	yogurt	Turkey
Bananas	Tomatoes	Cottage	Lean beef
Apples	Bell peppers	cheese	Fish
Pineapples	Carrots	String	Shrimp
Oranges	Zuchini	cheese	Deli meats
Melons	Broccoli	Milk (2%)	(no nitrates)
Grapes	Cauliflower	Eggs	
Rasberries	Onions	*Cheese	
Grapefruits	Spinach		
Key limes	Sweet potatoes		
	Greens (collard, turnips, swiss chard, kale, arugula)		

*Cheese – some healthy options: cottage, full-fat, organic, parmesan, swiss, feta

Grains
Wheat bread
Whole wheat pasta
Oatmeal (steel cut)
Quinoa
Ezekial bread
Lentils
Beans (explore the
varieties)
Brown rice

Snacks
Hummus
Popcorn
Nuts
Pita pockets
Raisins
Dark Chocolate
Salsa

Beverages
Water
Tea/coffee
Orange juice

Miscellaneous
Peanut butter	Olive oil	Canola oil	Hot sauce
Almond butter	Cooking spray	Vinegar	Agave nectar
Vegan mayo	Mustard	Honey	100 cal. snacks
Dried fruit	Monk sugar		

Exercise
Since we mentioned the impact that food can have on our bodies, it's only fitting to bring physical fitness to the party. Depending on your health condition and limitations, it's always best to start slow to prevent any form of injury to the body. As for me, exercise is challenging because I never know, on any given day, how my body is going to feel (I

definitely go from completely different spectrums). Some days I can hardly get out of bed because of the pain and extreme exhaustion; it's these days that I'm literally in bed all day and night and find it hard to find any enjoyment.

On the flip side, there are other days that I wake up feeling Grrrreat! It's on these days that I feel as if God has given me a reprieve, so I try to get in some form of light exercise, knowing not to overdo it because it will only have an adverse effect on my body. I usually start out by doing approximately 10-15 minutes of cardio (bike riding) and incorporate stretches throughout the day. On the days that my body won't allow any cardio, I do head-to-toe stretches and strength training modalities in bed, some in the morning and the remaining at night. **Rule #1 – Stop making excuses.**

It's key to know your body and not go beyond what it's capable of doing. If you're in good physical health but haven't worked out in a while, start out slow and gradually work up to adding additional 5–10 minute increments to your workout. As time progresses, you will find yourself working up to at least 30 minutes of physical activity each session. If you can do more, great but if not, don't beat yourself up. **Rule #2 – Know your limits.**

What's most important is that you get your heart rate up to at least 50% above your normal rhythm. Those who don't have any health challenges can shoot for a target of 70% higher than their normal heart rate, according to the American Heart Association (the chart varies according to age so do your research and see where you fit in).

The bottom line is, your heart is a muscle, and it needs physical activity just like the rest of the muscles in your body in order to pump blood effectively to all of its organs. Which brings me to **Rule #3 – Get that bootie moving** (talk to your doctor to see what your target rate should be if you are not sure).

"Getting the body in motion is not only beneficial in trimming your waistline. Being physically fit is also good for improved mental health and well-being, and it decreases your risk for cardiovascular disease, not to mention other health complications. So, what's the bottom line? If you're able to handle working out, health and vitality are sure to come. At the same time, if you want to shed a few pounds, focus on burning more calories than you consume; it's literally that simple, and don't forget to check that discipline!" (G. Poole).

Forgetting What's Behind

I remember sitting in my bedroom crying and wondering if my current marriage was going to make it. I, unfortunately, had brought tons of baggage from my previous relationship because I had not given myself enough time to heal from the past hurts. Thank You, Jesus! Because he gave me a gift named Julius Washington, who not only prayed for my crazy ass but also gave me the time I needed to figure it all out. I had put a band-aid on a cancerous wound that couldn't heal with my makeshift treatment. We eventually sorted it out together, which is why I can honestly say, you cannot do it alone.

When you're sinking in your own sorrows, it's almost as if you're drowning in your very own cesspool of quicksand. All the blaring signs are clearly there, along with the drama and intuition all around you that screams, HELP. However, if you don't set aside your pride and allow in those who are experienced and willing to assist, even though your vulnerability will be showing again, you lose. So, allow those around you to help you through the hurdles of life.

☀ My husband gave me this scripture for this section, and it fits perfectly. Philippians 3:13-14, **(13) Brothers and sisters, I don't consider that I have taken hold of it yet. But here is the one thing I do. I forget what is behind me. I push hard toward what is ahead of me. (14) I push myself forward toward the goal to win the prize. God has appointed me to win it. The heavenly prize is Christ Jesus himself.**

In any relationship, it's always best to start by not bringing any garbage along with you, or shall I say, eliminating the trash. This reminds me of a philosophical theory I learned many years ago while in college called Tabula Rasa. I don't know how I can remember some things and forget why I went into the kitchen, but whatever!

Anyway, the meaning behind this theory by philosopher John Locke is "blank slate." In short, it references how we're born without any built-in mental awareness, and that everything we pick up along the way is learned. I've learned that when you start any new relationship, you should begin without any preconceived notions; don't assume your new partner will be a carbon copy of your last one. Free yourself and learn to trust again.

Begin anew with the mindset that you will learn new things about yourself and your mate so that you can grow **together**. If by chance you're basing your current relationship off of your last one, then you're in serious trouble. The rule of thumb: God made each of us unique, and although we may have similar traits and characteristics, we're vastly different, as our thumbprints indicate.

If you happen to be suffering in your current relationship and haven't healed from the last one, take a step back and figure out what you've learned from the previous one and how that's shaped who you are today. It's more than okay for us to make mistakes, but it's not okay to wallow in the mess and take the other person down with us. Mistakes and disappointments happen; they're a part of life, and quite frankly, they are how we grow and mature.

For me, I guess I needed to know that it was safe or okay to be disappointed and to fall hard without a plan of correction. As a nurse and mother, I've learned to make a plan for just about every problem I've faced. However, during my downward spiral, things were very different, and for the first time in my life, I had no plan. This more than troubled me.

If you're stuck and find that you can't do it alone, **repair your mind and heart** by possibly going to counseling. Do it for yourself, and for goodness' sake, get rid of any stigmas associated with seeing a therapist, for your own mental health needs. If counseling isn't an option for you, try unleashing the fury with your Pastor, spiritual leader, or even close friend.

Here's what I have found to be true: when your mind and heart are troubled, that toxicity interferes with the very core of your life and way of thinking. If you're dealing with depression or riding the fence, you must find some way to lift the burdens that are weighing you down in a safe, constructive manner.

If you're not willing or able to do either of these, write the issues down. Writing is freeing; you don't have to worry about anyone judging you or anyone weighing in with their thoughts or opinions. Writing it all down allows you a voice without the intimidation or anxiety that may come with allowing yourself to be vulnerable. At the same time, start a prayer journal and attach scriptures that fit each particular problem. When your prayer(s) have been answered, record the date as well and mark it as, *Answered Prayer.*

By recording and tracking your progress, it will give you renewed strength and teach you how to praise God all the more (I actually learned this from Bishop Clark). When it's all said and done, these are testimonies that should be shared so that you can help someone else along the way, who may be going through the very same struggle you did. Shoe on the other foot – it's always good to know that you're not in this fight alone.

While you're doing these things, be sure you're communicating with our Heavenly Father who already knows the problem you're facing but wants to hear it from you. Why? Because He ultimately has all the answers, and He cares.

Proverbs 3:5-6, **Trust in the Lord with all your heart and lean not to your own understanding. In all your ways acknowledge Him and He will make your paths straight.** Meaning, when the chips are down and you can't seem to find your way, trust God. In other words, when you're unsure or doubtful, don't try to work it out on your own but trust and wait on God to provide the answer.

One more: Philippians 4:6-7, **Don't be anxious about anything, but in every situation with prayer and thanksgiving present your request to God. And the peace of God...will guard your hearts and your minds in Christ Jesus.** Plainly put, don't worry but be happy, because God is always on duty; He never takes a break.

So, the takeaway here is not to make your partner pay for past mistakes; it will only ruin your relationship and you in the process. Furthermore, if at all possible, do not take the junk or hurt into your new relationship. Give yourself time to heal and then forgive. Start with forgiving yourself and then forgive those who may have hurt you along the way. If left untreated, the hurt will, without a doubt, shift into autopilot. The way I view the untreated hurt(s) is like an infection, and the only antidote is forgiveness.

Forgiveness is the antibiotic taken for the infection, and without the necessary medicine, the infection runs rampant and infects its neighboring organs, and the result is ultimate destruction. Forgiveness is the salvation we all need; our part is to accept the challenge, and God does the rest.

Now that we know what love is and how to communicate with our mate, and have a working idea of what it will take to get our minds and bodies in shape, let's take a look at hygiene and grooming before we leap into our discussion about sex. Ladies, you're welcome!

Hygiene and Grooming

Ladies, if you want him groomed a certain way, tell him. I cannot stress enough how important it is to communicate all of your needs. If done properly, the dialogue will flow like the waves in the sea on a bright sunny day. That is, if you allow yourself to be vulnerable and tell your man or your boo how you like it – from hygiene to grooming, from dress to touch. How you want to be touched, caressed and, oh! the magnitude of the stroke, communicate that too. Go ahead and be his Delilah and manicure his beard, tell him how sexy he is, touch and caress his face. You must be all-in.

My mother was always a warden when it came to hygiene. I mean, her nose was and still is like a hound dog (my youngest son and I have inherited this gift as well) ready to sniff out its prey. You could not get a musty garment past my mom without a discussion about how to wash your arms... "Wash once to remove the soap and then a few more times to get the area clean." To take it a step further, she would demonstrate how to get the odor out of whatever caught her nose.

Similarly, Marmie (one of the names I call my mother) would always say, "Never leave the house without looking your best; you never know who you will run into." Over the years, I've adopted some of her quirks and added a few of my own practices that I've passed down to my children. The teeth, for example. I'm a stickler for clean teeth. I absolutely hate to see anyone's yucky tartar build-up – you know what I mean. They are talking to you with yellow gunk cased on their teeth, all the while smiling from ear to ear. People, gum disease is a real thing; it's especially important to floss and brush at least once a day – twice is best. Gum disease and poor dental hygiene can lead to heart disease; that too is a thing, people.

I hate to even write this next section down, but there are people out there that don't take hygiene seriously. Bathing is vital y'all (and I'll leave that one alone). Some aren't nit-picky, but washing your hair on a routine basis is necessary. And the teeth, well, we've already had that discussion, which leads us to the feet. If your feet are a little rough around the edges and odorous (you know who you are) do something about it. It's way too easy to wash your feet; scrub in between your toes and use a pumice stone to remove the dead skin. If for any reason you can't manage your own feet, go and see a podiatrist and/or a nail technician; that's what they're there for.

If you like going to the nail shop but are not confident in their cleaning practices, bring your own supplies because once you've come down with a fungal infection, it's hard to get rid of, and the medication that's prescribed internally is not good for you.

Bottom line: Don't wait until your spouse comments on *any* area of your body, but if that's what it takes, have the talk.

I'm just going to keep it all the way real. I have a problem with perspiration, especially now that I am menopausal. I'm so anal that I lift my arms and smell them throughout the day; I *do not* want to smell me, not in the least bit. Hmm…typing this is making me think I'm a bit OCD, but I'm sure my husband appreciates my body and, well, the honey pot being thoroughly cleansed. Although, he has been known to dip into my pot before I can make it to the bathroom. 🔆 Yes, I like it both ways.

When my husband and I met, he was clean-shaven, good enough to eat-smelling and looking good but, um…when we started dating, he started looking scruffy in the face. I would say, "Babe, can you shave?" and his reply was, "I like looking scruffy." We actually went back and forth a few times with this discussion until one day I told him that I liked the way he looked when he was trimmed up. I think I scored when I added that it turned me on. Now, although my husband hates shaving, he does shave more often than not, "Praise Be!"

At the same time, I remember him telling me that he liked my toes when they were polished. So, what that meant for me was, I had to keep my feet looking pretty. I even let him pick the color occasionally. My feet are always soft and ready to be admired. They're so supple, they can be used to stroke his body parts and are always ready to be massaged or sucked; whatever he wants to do, I'm ready! Okay, don't act like you don't like it. Of course you do, so keep them clean and manicured.

Okay, the vagina. Until now, I purposely skipped over this, but here we go. She is one fierce organ, and over the years, I've seen and heard of so many products to keep her clean, but in my opinion, they do an inadequate job of managing her insides. (She's a pronoun for now!) The vagina should be admired for all of her attributes; I mean, she not only delivers and receives pleasure, but she is the gateway through which babies travel. She's bad! But because of the hormones she secretes, she needs to be cleansed properly; you don't have to overdo it with creams, sprays and definitely not a douche to keep her tamed.

Treat her right. The vagina should be cleansed with plain soap and water, rinsed well and patted dry, that's it. Adding different things to the routine will most likely cause a change in the normal flora and ignite extra bacteria, thereby causing an unpleasant odor. The vagina on average is a pleasant-smelling organ but certain things can cause a change in the way she smells.

Some of those include menstruation, sexual intercourse, poor hygiene, certain materials (polyester, rayon, or silk) or leaving your pad or tampon in too long. Certain materials trap moisture and don't allow proper air flow to this valuable organ.

If you have an odor that is fishy (Lord, God!), well there is definitely a problem, and if you can't get rid of it by cleaning and changing your undergarments more frequently, you should definitely seek medical attention sooner rather than later. What's best are cotton-lined panties that allow the vaginal area to breath. If cotton panties aren't your thing, then changing more frequently is the next best option, but your girl needs ventilation, so maybe commando is for you.

The goal of good hygiene is, of course, individual, but you and your partner should be on the same page. You want to admire your mate; you want to be attracted to him or her sexually, so let them know what it is you desire. It's important that you have compassion and love when having this conversation because the last thing you want is for your partner to feel insecure with his or her body or with the way you view them.

If you like his face clean-shaven but are met with resistance, put on a nice panty set, wear his favorite scent, and plug in the clippers. If you like his penis cleaned before you have oral sex (yes, men this is a thing for some of us), then take a warm towel before and clean and stroke it before putting it into your mouth.

I mean, come on people, have some fun, lighten up. It is more than okay to use its anatomical names, even in casual conversation! Adam did! The takeaway from this section is to be honest and clear with your mate. Allow him or her to know what your preferences are and why. Prayerfully, the two of you will be able to meet in the middle, making both of you happy and ready for the next sexual encounter.

Chapter 6 – *Sex, Oh La-La*
(There's More Than Meets the Eye)

Is Oral Sex, Sex?

I've heard this question posed many times throughout my adult life and depending on who's answering the question, you just may get a different answer. Studies have shown that teens and young adults don't actually classify oral sex as sex at all. And well, I even put it in my mind that I wasn't having sex with my now-husband before we got married, but in all actuality, we were definitely indulging in sexual activity. I believe the misconception lies with insertion.

Most people see sex and/or sexual intercourse as one and the same, but there's a slight difference, y'all. Intercourse suggests penetration with the glorious penis into the vagina. Well, okay then, let's just take a look at some actual definitions.

Sex – Sexual activity, including specifically sexual intercourse.

Sexual intercourse – Sexual activity typically involving insertion and thrusting of the penis.

Sexual activity – Any activity, singular or between two persons, that induces sexual arousal.

Oral sex – Sexual activity in which the genitals of one partner are stimulated by the mouth of another; stimulating your partner's genitals with your mouth, lips or tongue.

So, every time we used our lips, mouths and tongues on each other's genitals before marriage, we were actually having sex. WHAT?! I had totally rationalized that we were definitely not having sex because there was no penetration going on. I didn't learn this classification in high school, and it wasn't a topic in nursing school. So, I was just as ignorant as those who viewed oral sex as no sex at all, but we now know it's a fallacy; they're wrong. Oral sex is sex, and it's great, I might add. Amen! And who knows, at some point, it may be added as one of the wonders of the world.

For those who don't partake, I must say, *you are missing out, my friend.* I know that it may seem as if that doesn't go there (the penis in the mouth or the mouth on the vagina), but with that view, that's why you're missing out. And for those who are just on the receiving end, well again, y'all are missing out too! I don't know what it is, but when I'm engaged in oral sex, it completely intensifies the whole sexual experience. *Wait*! How is that?

Just think about it, if oral sex was taken off the table, it would be like having an ice cream sundae without the cherry, like having rice without gravy, or awaiting a sermon without the preacher. You see, those missing elements are necessary, not to be overlooked or omitted, just like oral sex is a necessary sexual experience, not to be removed or unincorporated.

I mean, sure, you would still have kissing, which is great. I love to kiss. You'd still have touching the genitals, which is also an incredible experience if done right – only if done right, I must add. This is why you ladies need to speak up and tell your man **how** and **when**.

You also have your audible experiences. Music perhaps can set the stage; it's not only relaxing if you put on some old-school R&B love songs. You know them, the slow jams; hip-thrusting modulations with the right words, it will get you in the right mood so you can rock with it. Also, the words we say and the tone in which we say them can literally make your genitals skip a beat and feel as if there's a heartbeat in there. So, imagining sex without oral sex, in my opinion, isn't a complete sexual experience, to put it plainly.

My husband apparently knows when to switch his high sounds into a Barry White, show you right! He must know that when he gets close to my ear and starts complimenting the way I look, the way I feel and then switches to "How does this feel?" yep, he's got me at that point and the honey pot has been moistened before he's even done anything physical. It must be those 13 years of life experience he has on me. He must have troubleshooted or weeded out every failed attempt and/or experience because he knows exactly what to do and when to do it. Hallelujah!

I told him that he needs to teach a course. It should be entitled "How to Make Her Moan" because every woman should have the opportunity to feel as I do. This man takes his time, and it feels as if he's running plays on me, setting me up for the big touchdown. All of these experiences formulate into a wonderous sexual experience, all of them together, not leaving our friend oral sex out. It puts a period there, signaling a stand-alone moment, nothing else necessary to complete it. Put a fork in it because you will be done, especially if you have all the elements on your plate.

If by chance you haven't dabbled in the oral arena, give it at least the old college try. How about once for good measure? So, sex as a stand-alone act is, yes, sensational without a doubt. But when oral sex comes to the party, there's no party like an oral sex party cause the oral sex party, it **tops**. Ok, just talking about it makes me happy and has me wanting to sing. And that is just what happens to me when my husband goes south. I don't know if it's his hands, his magical tongue, his soft lips or that damn genius brain of his that knows exactly how to manipulate my body into getting in line with his. Maybe it's all of the above because I can't seem to sing his praises enough.

It's always different, never routine, and always a pleasurable moment. It's long too, thank You, Jesus! Yes, I can say, "Thank You, Jesus" because He made our bodies to be loved in this way. Anyway, whatever your heart so desires, as long as the two of you agree, there's nothing off the table, **really**. God wanted us to enjoy the total sexual experience, which is why He made us loving beings with a sexual desire. Lol! I have to laugh about this because there are so many thank you Jesus moments in our love-making experience. I used to feel weird about it or thought my husband would feel some sort of way about me shouting it out, but I've learned to go with the flow (he also occasionally gives Him a shout-out). I just know that God wants us to give Him praise and to thank Him for ALL things, and we do.

Anyway, getting back to my fabulous husband, I don't know which tactic he uses that I would call my favorite because they're all wonderful. I mean, I love, love when he does what I call a figure eight on my clitoris. Can you imagine? I also enjoy when he lightly strokes my outer labia with his tongue, sort of teasing me but not diving in; it drives me darn crazy.

And, oh! How I adore when he strokes my labia like a popsicle, taking jabs at my clitoris – yes! – all the while penetrating my vagina. It's totally incredible. But then, there are other times that I don't even know what in the hell he's doing down there and have to literally take a look. It's in those moments that I feel as if I'm having an out-of-body experience; no one else is at the party except me, and all I can say is, "WOW."

Well, even though very long-winded, I said all of that to say that oral sex is definitely sex. So, the next time someone asks you if you are having sex (and there's no intercourse happening), take a moment and give a wonderful grin as you answer, "Hell yeah."

Masturbation

I know that some of you won't admit to it, but I cannot think of a person that hasn't masturbated. If you are a guy, well then, everyone knows you definitely jerk off or masturbate from time to time. However, when it comes to women, masturbation is looked at as a sinful act. I know that there are some spiritual leaders who will say that masturbation is morally wrong and there's some controversy around the topic, but I've never actually seen or heard of a scripture that aligns with that notion. Instead, I've only heard that it is against God.

Masturbation, by way of definition, is the erotic stimulation of one's own genitals, commonly resulting in an orgasm, or in short, touching yourself for sexual pleasure. We learn at a young age that touching the genital area elicits a different response than touching any other part of the body, resulting in gratification or pleasure. We also learn that touching this area releases tension; it calms us down and puts us in a better overall state of mind. I remember being a young child and being scolded for self-touch. I, in turn, did the very same thing to my children, not knowing that it was a normal part of a child's development to explore.

As for the Bible, well, there are certain scriptures that inform of immoral acts but not specifically pertaining to masturbation. Let me check with my husband and pastor of our home... The Bible does not discuss masturbation or say it's a sin. But we should probably do it with our mate in mind.

Thanks, honey!

It's amazing to me that this simple form of touch to your own body can cause so much tension, division, and hostility in the world, even today. Dr. Joycelyn Elders, a professor of pediatrics at the University of Arkansas, who also served as the first African American Surgeon General in 1993 but was later forced to resign after her discussion on masturbation in 1994.

I mean, really?! This doctor was talking about safe sex strategies to help prevent the spread of AIDS and other STDs. Where was freedom of speech then, or the simple fact that Dr. Elders was 100% correct in what she was saying? The fact remains that the topic of masturbation makes some individuals feel uncomfortable and splits the brains of even some of the most brilliant minds, even though they themselves indulge in this act (shame on them).

Masturbation is a normal and healthy practice that both partners should explore, not to mention talk about. Truth be told, it is a wonderful way to get to know your body and help your partner understand what makes you tick. How can your husband or wife know what makes you feel good unless you actually explore it for yourself (rub-a-dub-dub)? No one knows your body better than you so go ahead and touch the tip of the iceberg and don't be afraid or ashamed in any way. God is not going to get you or condemn you to Hell; if it were so, it would be in the Good Book, and we've already established that it's not.

Once you know what area turns you on, the exact amount of pressure, or if you like to insert, go and tell it on the mountain, or better yet, tell your mate. Your spouse will thank you for it in the long run because they ultimately want to know how to please you. Even better, have him or her watch; it's a total turn-on. What do you have to lose?

I remember my husband showing me how he liked his penis rubbed or stroked. The mere act of watching him do it, although he was teaching me, that alone, made me sopping wet, and I could hardly wait to touch him and do it myself.

I also remember a time when I started rubbing my breast and then started masturbating while he watched. He told me that he was completely turned on and how much he enjoyed it; that addition completely heightened the sexual experience. So, all I'm saying is, try it out before you lie to yourself and others and say you don't do it or don't like it. Don't be a closet keeper (a person who says something is wrong but actually performs the act). Free yourselves.

Do You Enjoy Sex; If Not, Why?

This is a question most people don't ask, but it's believed that most enjoy the act of sex, right? Wrong. There are instances where men and women don't find enjoyment in love-making at all. Some reasons can either be physical or psychological, but whatever the reason, some couples find themselves detached from the idea of intimacy and sex. These things should be communicated to each other, and ultimately, the issue should be brought to a medical professional for exploration or causation.

Sometimes, couples that have been married for a long time lose the thrill or the enjoyment they once shared, and sex then is taken off the table. The excitement for some dies down and/or the act becomes so routine and boring that it is no longer fun or enjoyable.

Furthermore, with advancing age comes physical problems with the body that can spill over into many couples' sex lives. When the two are having physical or psychological problems, the stress associated with not performing causes the act of sex to decrease or altogether be removed. But when the problem affects just one individual, it then affects the couple as a whole. This stress can put the relationship in jeopardy because the relationship then becomes one-sided, and in this scenario, understanding and compassion aren't always aligned.

Because a woman's body is constantly changing, there will be times when we choose not to engage in sexual relations. These reasons can stem from childbirth, menstruation, menopause, pain and/or psychological issues, all of which can make us have an aversion to sex, but I'm here to tell you there is hope.

Normal occurrences in a woman's body are not problematic because they have an expected end that both partners can wrap their heads around. The problems, however, come into play when we are dealing with ongoing issues or health problems that seem never-ending. The uncertainty of our situation can cause emotional havoc, and if our problems aren't communicated properly, it can cause unnecessary strain and thus never be resolved.

So, can we say we enjoy sex when we're overwhelmed with medical issues? Can we say we enjoy sex when our partner seems distant or when we have body image issues? Or can we then say we enjoy sex when we cannot remember the last occurrence?

Getting into the reasons why we change our perspective on sex likely stems from a past occurrence or perception regarding sex. What are your views on sex and how does it make you feel? Do you feel uncomfortable in any way when the subject is broached? If so, ask yourself why. Sex or making love should be enjoyable and not a chore. One should find fulfillment when making love to their spouse. I mean, that is the basis of it: love! Right?

God created man to love and to be loved. Making love should be natural and should be the additive that propels your love, igniting passion over and over again. If you can't remember the last time you made love to your spouse, chances are there's no intimacy going on. If there's no intimacy, then you have one or both partners who are operating in want and are not being fulfilled, which is a dangerous zone to be in.

Here's the Fix

Communicate to the moon and back about your feelings, even if you *think* your partner knows them. Sometimes when we speak, depending on the amount of information being given at that time, there are things that may get misconstrued or lost in translation. So, it's worth saying it again. Lose that frustration that may be associated with repetitive communication.

If your schedules are posing a problem, set aside some time, and put a date on the calendar. ☼ We put dates on the calendar for vacations and other things that are important to us, so why not set aside a specific time for your mate? I know that this may seem to be an extra step, but trust me, setting aside time for the two of you to work on your relationship – a chance to build the framework of love – is more than worth it. Actually, having a definite date to work on matters of the heart will allow you to hold each other accountable for repairing the areas of breakdown in the relationship. Likewise, it is also sending the message that your relationship is worth it.

If pain is the issue, by all means, medicate prior, whether prescription or over the counter. As for me, I give myself at least 30 minutes to get my pain level down or into a controllable range. You can also try a warm, Epsom salt bath and light some candles to relax your body; it will help relieve any stress and help in reducing muscle pain.

Creams work as well to relieve certain types of pain. You can try to apply the cream an hour before the bath to allow it time to penetrate the skin. Most pain-relieving creams and sprays are very odorous so giving it time to work before your bath will actually help the body relax further, with an element of pain relief. I've actually tried this technique and it seems to work fairly well if you have arthritic pain. Don't apply arthritic creams directly after a bath (wait until your body cools down) because your pores are wide open, and it will be quite the sting.

My father had given me an arthritic cream to try once, and I applied it after my bath for pain relief. Boy, was I in for a shock. My back and hips were burning so much, I couldn't keep still. It literally felt as if the areas of application were on fire (it had capsaicin in it). The only thing that relieved the burn was neutralizing shampoo, it was rapid fix.

Do your research and don't stop experimenting with various creams or sprays, etc. in your quest for pain management. Lastly, make sure that you are stretching regularly to allow your muscles to remain loose. Tight muscles and joints will increase the intensity of the pain. Finally, talk to your medical provider and/or therapist if you've tried what you think is everything and nothing seems to work. Enjoyable sex requires both mental and physical participation, so perhaps your physician can help.

Try a variety of things to see what works best for you. You might even try intimacy exercises to help bring back the spark in your relationship so sex can be part of the team again.

Intimacy Exercises Without Sex (Without Sex? What Is She Talking About?)

1. Try timed kissing, lips only. Start off with 2-3 minutes, use your phone to track the time and have fun.
2. Do some timed kissing in other places, i.e., neck, fingers, ears etc. with your partner blindfolded; this adds an element of seduction.
3. Bring something from the kitchen to kiss or lick off of your partner – you pick. (i.e., pudding, yogurt, maple syrup, whipped cream)
4. Give a body massage with warm oil. Add soft music and candles.
5. Go for a walk and hold hands. Talk to each other; leave the problems or drama out of it.
6. Do something nice and unexpected for your spouse without wanting anything in return. (i.e., cooking,

cleaning, shopping or a special gift from their favorite store)

7. Bring sex into the conversation. What are their likes and dislikes, hindrances if any, what are their fantasies?

The purpose of doing these exercises is to get more familiar and comfortable with your partner. Even if you've been in a relationship for some time, you can still benefit from these exercises (you know far less than you think).

The fact is, we are ever-evolving, and the same is true of our needs. And as time goes on, if we're not careful we can begin to take the other person for granted. So, doing an ongoing assessment of needs and wants, keeping an ongoing dialogue, is necessary to maintain a healthy and happy relationship.

As your relationship progresses, there may be times when you will know the thing(s) that makes your partner tick, but for some reason or another, neglect them because you get caught up in the hustle and bustle called life (work, business, kids, you know).

To stay on top of everything, let your partner know how much you care about them; how valuable they are. I hate to put this on the table, but life is so precious; none of us knows when our last day is going to be, so be kind, loving and treat each day as if it were your last. Just so that you end up on top, with no regrets, let your actions speak for themselves; words alone won't always cut it, meaning they are not always enough. Make your relationship a priority if you're not already doing so. You can rekindle the love and begin to feel alive again if only you *try*.

"So, can I love my mate and not want to have sex?"
Yes! Here is a list of reasons why some people may
not enjoy sex:

- They have difficulty being aroused or it takes longer to excite them or get them in the mood.
- Obesity or feeling uncomfortable with changes in the body.
- Aversion to sex (possibly related to sexual abuse or trauma),
- Inability to achieve an orgasm (20% of women have never achieved an orgasm).
- Painful sex (due to arthritis, endometriosis, menopause or related to a lack of estrogen).
- Erectile dysfunction, early ejaculation or premature ejaculation.
- Enlarged prostate (blood flow inhibited to the penis equals impotence).
- Smoking (can impair sexual performance and lead to erectile dysfunction).
- Physical conditions such as overall poor health, diabetes, heart disease, high blood pressure and anxiety, just to name a few.
- Some medications taken can sometimes cause sexual dysfunction, so talk to your doctor to see what the origin is.

Erectile Dysfunction and Our Story

When dealing with any medical condition that impairs the ability to have sex, you should know that there are various treatment options out there, so don't give up. Whether it's incorporating physical therapy or psychotherapy, modification of your diet, incorporating exercise or mediation, don't despair because you can still have incredible sex. The key to turning things around is to not give up. When one thing doesn't work, keep trying until you get the results you desire.

I can attest to this because my husband and I have had our fair share of difficulties when it comes to erectile dysfunction, hence struggles with having sex, but neither of us has ever stopped trying to figure it out or exploring to find the right avenue that works best for us. Not in any particular order but, in the past, we've tried creams, gels, pills, pumps and injections – yes injections.

Sure, all of it can be frustrating, not to mention overwhelming when trying to figure it all out, especially for the affected individual. The initial thought is that the first thing you try is going to be the thing that works, and when it doesn't, it's more than disappointing, to say the least.

Just a suggestion, always start with the least invasive way of managing any problem and then work your way up from there. As a nurse and patient, I've discovered that not all treatment plans will work the same for every patient. Everyone's body composition, not to mention lifestyle, is different, which is why there are so many products on the market today trying to meet the needs of those dealing with E.D. and other similar issues.

It's funny now, even hilarious, when we reminisce (my husband and I still chuckle to this day). I can vividly remember trying the penis pump as if it were yesterday, and all the issues and pain surrounding it. It's a cylindrical plastic device that slips over the head of the penis. First, you place a rubber/silicone ring onto the penis and slide it to the base (can you imagine sliding this rubber ring and snagging all of the pubic hairs along the way? Ouch!). The ring works in conjunction with the cylindrical tube that eventually makes a seal over the entire penis.

Although this situation isn't funny, it is making me laugh right now because my husband would make this comment, "Babe, when I tell you to stop pumping you always say, one more," and boy, was he right. I actually wanted to see just how big his penis could get. Which brings me to the next step.

So, the last action in making this pump work seemed like magic: inflating the device. There's a pump that attaches to the chamber, similar to the one on a blood pressure cuff, and all you have to do is keep squeezing the ball until you get the desired length or effects.

I mean, that device did its job. I can see it now, as his penis grew by leaps and bounds – I mean, OMG, it was really big. I was so amazed, not to mention ready to get that contraption off his penis so we could give it a try. It took some adjusting, finding the desired size and/or firmness while manipulating the pump, but getting that rubber ring off was a nightmare.

I honestly felt horrible when we tried to remove the ring; the look of anguish on his face was awful. Ultimately, the penis pump just wasn't for us because even though we had penetration, what he had to endure just wasn't worth it in the end. Also, the hard-on didn't last long enough to make up for the barbaric preparation we had to go through. So, what that meant for us was, on to the next treatment option!

We also tried testosterone gel, and when that wasn't effective, we upgraded to the extended-release patches that were applied directly onto his chest wall and/or his back. After his brain surgery and subsequent radiation treatments, his body was deficient in many ways and could no longer produce the necessary hormones, one being testosterone (lab test revealed levels that were almost non-existent).

With regular treatments, we noticed more energy, improved cognition and increased desire to have sex again. That in of itself was a miracle, in my opinion. However, the topical hormones did not raise his levels high enough, so we had to transition to bi-monthly injections that we do at home. Having your own nurse at home has its advantages, right? Even though the hormones are now at a good level, they didn't fix our main issue with erectile dysfunction, so it was on to the next treatment options:

Testosterone – a vital (predominantly male) hormone secreted in the body; men secrete approximately 50% more than women. So, what does it do?

- Brain: increases mental awareness, increases mood and confidence, is responsible for sex drive and aids in memory.
- Bone: increases bone density.
- Muscles: increases strength, muscle mass and endurance.
- Bone marrow: produces red blood cells.

- Sex organs: responsible for sperm production, erectile function, prostate growth and strong erections.
- Skin: produces body and facial hair.

Prescription Medication – The oral medications to treat E.D. work by increasing the blood supply to the penis. We've tried two different oral medications, at varying doses, and they worked to some degree, but we didn't find them beneficial in the end. If you find yourself in this grey area of not knowing what to do next, hang in there and don't allow the frustrations to win.

Men all over the world have this similar problem and what works for one may not work for the other. Just be encouraged and know that there are oral medications that work well for some individuals. All I can say is, be patient because nothing is an instant fix. At the same time, with this group of medications, you have to work for what you want, almost like football players do, building their plays for the ultimate touchdown. Stimulation of the mind and body are necessary, as well as some 5-digit manipulation on your part to be successful.

So be creative in setting the stage as well as the mood because it helps things progress in terms of an erection taking place. Learn to implement foreplay and change it up sometimes; don't make it routine every time, **boring**. With the oral medication, my husband was able to have an erection, but it wasn't consistent, a complete bummer! I remember it being frustrating for both of us, but again, we didn't lose hope. So, say it with me, **on to the next treatment option!**

Our last treatment in our battle over erectile dysfunction was the injections. Bingo! I must say that the first time we went in for a trial run was completely amazing. I was like, "You is big, you is strong, and you is going inside of me!" (Okay, if you haven't seen The Help, that won't be as comical). I mean, for real, after we left the doctor's office, we made a pit stop to the bathroom at Kaiser Hospital to have a quicky. It was totally me that forced his hand, I mean really. And we scccooorrreddd! We still have a laugh about that incident today.

Now this injectable medication (a compound medication involving more than one drug) that we first used was definitely successful in maintaining an erection for an extended period of time. I mean, I've never, never, ever, ever, ever had sex for longer than 20 minutes, nope, never. Well, this medication will have you going back for seconds, thirds, fourths and even for dessert. Because of its effectiveness, my husband has been known to wake me up after I'm in my post-sex sleep phase and start it up all over again. I would say lucky me, but it's really all about him at that point.

Of course, I'm exaggerating by saying this, but I'm surprised his penis didn't fall off during our trial period with this medication. Please hear me when I say that being engorged for more than four hours truly means that you should be heading to the emergency room for the antidote or maybe even to get it drained. But because my husband is as stubborn as a mule, he always refused. Having a penis hard for an extended period can leave men with damage to the penis wall, affecting the shape and even causing permanent E.D. with no possible treatment options available. My husband was blessed in that area of not having any damage during our trial-and-error phase. Since then, we've learned to figure it out without making that trip; he's a horrible patient, but I'm sure 8 out of 10 men are as well.

So, although this first medication was great for me, it wasn't completely successful for him because he had pain associated with achieving an erection during and after sex. And when we found the right dose to make it a rockstar, we just couldn't get it to go down in a sufficient amount of time.

Tips for couples going the injection route:

1. Practice the injections on a banana, using tap water.
2. Order a 31-gauge needle; the 29g which they will give you will hurt (in our experience).
3. Know that the prescribed dose may or may not be appropriate when starting out. This is the trial-and-error period.
4. Talk to your doctor about injecting half the medication first and see how the penis responds because once you inject the full dose, it's really a waiting game as to how long the penis will remain hard.
5. If the penis is hard longer than the desired or recommended time, try eliminating (go pee), taking a shower and walk around. Adding these elements, not to mention the upright position have been known to help it go down.
6. What our doctor recommended was a nasal spray to have around to treat priapism (an erection that lasts too long). Pseudoephedrine can be purchased over the counter. Talk to your doctor about this medication during your visit and about all options that could go wrong.
7. Go to the emergency room if all else fails, especially if you want to maintain the use and function of your penis.

We ultimately switched doctors and the new urologist had a different compound form that was perfect without the other side effects. (And the crowd cheers, "Hooray!" Okay, that was just in my mind). Another hurdle with the injectable medication, like I mentioned earlier, was finding the right needle size. Trial and error is all I have to suggest, but it was extremely painful initially until we discovered a higher gauge needle (the higher the gauge, the smaller the diameter of the needle), meaning less pain at the injection site.

Erectile dysfunction is a quite common disorder that affects millions of men each year and therefore couples across the world. For my husband and me, this problem came from a diagnosis of prostate cancer and the treatment to remove the affected cells. When anyone is faced with a diagnosis like cancer, the least of their worries is whether they will be able to perform sexually. This realization about sex comes much later, after the stress of the cancer is removed, and the patient begins to see life as an option again. Because we've lived this unfortunate experience, I can honestly say that our love has stood the test of time and is stronger because of it, in every way possible.

For many couples, performance, or the inability to maintain an erection creates mayhem in the relationship, and this can leave both partners with feelings of inadequacy. The bigger problem, however, is that some individuals begin to isolate themselves, some stray and unfortunately others find themselves facing divorce over the issue of impotence and intimacy. Hopefully, through our story, we can give hope to couples around the world facing these same or similar challenges.

What if a Full Erection Doesn't Happen? What Can We Do?

I think it's noteworthy to understand that just because a full erection doesn't take place, the man still has a great desire and need to be intimate with you. Please don't think for one minute that the connection is broken or shouldn't happen. Take the time to love on one another, yes, even without an erection. Think about it, what do you like, what does he like? Then see how you can achieve satisfaction; it can totally take place.

Here are some things we've tried when we weren't successful in that aspect:

1. Continue with foreplay. As we've discussed, foreplay is a wonderful way to stay connected in love. And you can actually assist your partner in achieving satisfaction.
2. Watch or assist your partner in masturbation.
3. Have oral sex. Oral sex provides stimulation to the sex organ so that excitation and of course an erection or orgasm can take place.
4. Caress each other and provide reassurance that you're there with your partner for the long haul.
5. We haven't tried this just yet, but if a full erection doesn't take place, you can use a vibrator or dildo to provide vaginal stimulation, in lieu of the penis.

We make love with more than our bodies but also with our minds, so be all-in.

In essence, it really doesn't matter the cause, why you got there, but the solution in this situation is to build a stronger bond emotionally. It's to communicate your desires and needs, and in turn, seek the advice of a medical professional that can help you work through your issues. The problem of erectile dysfunction can be treated in many men out there; couples just need to be patient with one another and with their medical provider to find the best treatment option. At the same time, couples need to stay the course and not give up until they are completely satisfied with their care plan.

If your needs are not being met by your current doctor or if you're not being heard, get a second opinion, or change physicians because no one should suffer in this way, especially when there are so many treatment options available.

The takeaway in this section is to first figure out your goals and then consult with your doctor about your options. Just know that you may need to switch things along the way: oral medication, creams, injections or whatever you opt to use. Sometimes the body can have an adverse reaction along the way or not have the initial result of maintaining an erection, so don't panic if this happens to you. Rest assure and know that you are not in this fight alone; there are couples across the globe going through similar situations. So, no need to be ashamed, feel awkward or embarrassed about communicating your needs. Everyone has their own set of unique challenges to deal with along the way. *You've got this*!

So, What Are the Benefits of Sex?

I love the closeness that's shared between my husband and me when we're making love; it's almost magical. This closeness doesn't dissipate after making love but lingers for hours, even days, making me want him more and more. We laugh more, kiss more and are in each other's presence all the time. It's a joyous time. Could this be why the Bible says to have sex often? Well, I personally think so. At the same time, this was one of the first commands given to Adam and Eve, to have sex.

Genesis 1:28 NIV, **God blessed them and said to them, "Be fruitful and increase in number."**

You see, the more we make time for love-making, the more in tune we are with each other. When we have sex, there are hormones that are secreted from the brain (dopamine, oxytocin and vasopressin) that make us happy; they help make us physically, emotionally, and sexually attracted to our mate. These hormones tell us we want **more**. They make us want to cuddle and bond with our mates, all the while strengthening our bond.

Here are some benefits of having sex:
- Good for your cardiovascular health
- Lowers blood pressure
- Relieves stress
- Decreases overall pain
- Improves sleep
- Decreases depression and increases mood
- Increases pleasure
- Boosts self-esteem
- Reproduction

Where Is Your Mind?

One would think that when we're in the intimate act of making love that we're only thinking of him or her, right? Unfortunately, that's not always the case. I can recall several instances where I completely drifted off, thinking about menial things like what to cook for the next meal, writing options, or who I needed to call. I mean, I can literally get into deep thoughts, and boy, do they come out of nowhere.

I literally have to re-direct my thought process, forcing me to switch gears in order to sometimes stay on track. If you don't change or re-direct your thinking, it is totally possible that an orgasm may not happen at all, or that the overall experience won't be the best, leaving you thinking, "What in the world just happened?" Switch into pleasure gear and be mindful about your thoughts. Think about what is going on, or what's going **in**, for that matter. Talk to your partner about the experience or make small talk to allow your brain to shift gears or focus; even mindful groans will help in this situation.

It's not that farfetched of an idea, that we can't keep our thoughts in line with our actions because of how busy we are, not to mention the stressed, fast-paced lives we lead. So, when stepping into an intimate act like making love, even though we want nothing more than to give of ourselves, it's sometimes hard to switch gears or turn off that element that's distracting us in our minds.

It reminds me of the song "Your Body's Here With Me (But Your Mind's on the Other Side of Town)" by the O'Jays. The song's lyrics describe a person who's not completely vested in the relationship and is seeing someone else, and expresses how it makes that person feel when two lovers aren't on the same page, so to speak.

You see, when one spouse isn't in it to win it, the balance is ultimately thrown off. You can fake an orgasm (but why would you want to?), but you can't continue to pretend to be in love or to want to love your spouse. Because the mind and the body are connected, it just doesn't work if the mind is somewhere else. And if you're truly connected, the other person can feel the level of loss or misconnection. Without being in tune or totally connected, the sparks are minimal or completely non-existent . But, oh yeah, when you have that Wonder Twin power and the two align, that's when the magic happens, it's when sparks fly and you're all bubbly and giddy inside.

So, what do you do when the two of you are out of sync and desperately want to be on the same page? Here are a few things that you can do to forget about all of your troubles and your nine to five... and just sail on. Since this book also focuses on building our relationships so you can have amazing sex, try these options:

- Make an emotional connection – Be intentional about your daily conversations and actions. Make a valiant effort to get to know your partner. Find out what makes them happy/sad and learn to pick up on the non-verbal cues (until you figure them out, ask what they mean). Be vulnerable, let those walls down and learn to be the friend you need and want.
- Meditate together – Take the time to be quiet, mentally and physically. You can do this by sitting back-to-back or lying shoulder to shoulder where you can feel each other's breath. Meditation is a time of removing any negativity; it's a time to build mental strength and clarity so that you can get you back on track.

- Make time for each other – Don't let a day or week go by without carving out time for your mate. People get up extra early every day just to make it to work on time. They go out of their way to be an exceptional employee, to get marked reviews and accolades, so why not work just as hard, if not harder, on your relationship?

  You can't have favorable outcomes without putting in the hard work. If you make an effort to keep the flame burning, you won't have to go into crisis mode when there's a problem. Keep the structure solid and do the repairs along the way to keep the foundation strong. A touch-up here and there will keep you from purchasing a new building, and a relationship follows the same principle.

- Take a look back – Go through old photos and/or videos, pull out those old cards or letters and talk about the times when the two of you met or had an exceptional time together. Take the necessary time to laugh and reflect. Life is truly too short not to. Remember how you got to the place you are now and possibly mimic those actions as a way to rebuild or strengthen the relationship. My husband and I will occasionally watch our wedding video just to see the love and laughter we had for one another. We definitely love each other more today, but it's just another way to keep the love alive.

- Learn to smile more – Why go through your day looking like Oscar the Grouch from Sesame Street? If there's a problem, try to fix it quickly and bring your partner in to be the glue or the support you need.

Whenever I have a problem, I don't hesitate to share it with my husband. I don't always need a resolution to the problem, but I need an ear to vent to. In this way, he can help me instead of me trying to figure it out or carrying the burden alone. God instituted marriage so that we would not have to do it alone, so that we can tackle life as a team. He did it for US. When I think of smiling even in the face of adversity, one of the things that comes to mind is music. Music is the perfect way to put a smile on your face. These songs fit perfectly (partial lyrics).

"Smile" by Nat King Cole:

Smile though your heart is aching
Smile even though it's breaking
When there are clouds in the sky, you'll get by
If you smile through your fear and sorrow
Smile and maybe tomorrow
You'll see the sun come shining through for you

"Smile" by Kirk Franklin:

When I think how much better I'm gonna be when this
is over
I smile, even though I hurt see I smile
I know God is working so I smile
Even though I've been here for a while
I smile, smile
It's so hard to look up when you been down
Sure would hate to see you give up now
You look so much better when you smile, so smile

- Talk about it – Holding it in only creates more stress and drama in the relationship, not to mention worry, so let it out.
- Watch a movie or video – My husband and I will sometimes watch a video that he made on his phone from a previous love encounter (with me, of course), as a way to get us in the mood. You see, there are times when one partner may not be quite there, so watching a video or movie will change your mind frame and get you in that sexual mood.
- If you don't have any love shots, make them. Making videos will enhance your mood to another level. Try it. I promise you won't regret it. When making a video, you're in charge and can dictate the positions, the clothes, music or not and the length. Have fun with it!

Being Busy and Finding Intimacy

Whether it's that you have children and can't seem to find time for one another, have a stressful job and work endless hours, or if the two of you seem to fly by like strangers in the night, **stop** and do an assessment of your situation to get your relationship back on track. It is totally fixable. Life will go on with or without you; that's the reality of the situation. But **if** God has joined the two of you together, don't you at least owe it to yourselves to see why?

I've learned that anything worth having involves an incredible amount of work. And sometimes, even though that effort may be grueling, it's imperative that you do the work before your marriage is destroyed. Even if it feels like the love is gone and there's no coming back from the fiery pit, TRY, and give your marriage the fighting chance that it so deserves.

And if you are thinking that you're going to just wait until the kids have left the coup, well, it will be even harder later. Once the kids are grown and gone, if you haven't been actively working on your marriage, you will then find yourselves as strangers, not knowing who the other is or which way is up. You can't go years without knowing each other and think 20 years down the road, you'll be best friends. It just doesn't work like that.

Again, it is never too late to start over or to create a new chapter in the relationship called love; some just don't actually know where to start. Some individuals think marriage is easy and they get into the relationship without putting in the time. But ultimately, they end up drifting by each day without a concept of what they are doing.

Let me see if I can make this any clearer. If you had a child and left him or her on their own to figure things out and never actually nurtured them, they would grow wild. However, if you take that child by the hand and teach them everything they need to know to be successful in life, they flourish.

Well, the same principle applies to marriage or any relationship you're in. You must enter that union knowing that you have to put something in (make a deposit) every day. Just like a plant requires water and nutrients to survive, so does any relationship or marriage. Whenever you get thrown off track, and trust me it will happen, take a step back or time out to come together and discuss the problem areas. Sometimes with kids and a busy workload, the relationship gets lost, but you have to carve out some time; even if it's 10-15 minutes a day, grab it and give your spouse that undivided attention and time. It will literally save your marriage.

So, what does this look like? Well, say that you're both home from work, tired and ready to wind down. Dinner needs to be made and he's on the couch. Well, take five minutes to freshen up, get out of those work clothes and into something comfortable, possibly even sexy attire. Whether it's stretchy pants and a t-shirt without a bra, a mid-length nighty or one of his t-shirts, the point is to unwind and relax. Then, go and sit on his lap or straddle him, applying pressure where needed, and lightly give him a kiss – not a smack but give him some tongue. Then, go about your evening routine, and I promise he'll be thinking of you. And to change it up, here are some examples to get you away from your routine.

- You can set up a cocktail on the porch or patio after the kids are asleep.
- Run a bath for the two of you with candles.
- Put on some music and dance like you did when the two of you met.
- Create a space for a picnic in your home and have dinner on the floor instead of at the table.

When thinking of your own ways, try and create an atmosphere of pleasure.

Chapter 7 - *Prayer Works!*

Pray it Through

The Bible tells us to pray without ceasing because there are going to be difficult times in life when you feel like giving up and throwing in the towel. It's at those critical points that you need to stay committed to trusting God, being hopeful and not focusing on your feelings because those feelings will throw you all the way off and make you misinterpret the situation.

Proverbs 3:5 says, **Trust in the Lord with all your heart and lean not to your own understanding, acknowledge Him in all your ways and He will make your path straight.**

You see, the enemy doesn't want the commitment of marriage to function or run smoothly, so the feelings of hope and despair need to be put in check and given to the one who is able to solve them. There will always be something that will make you think the relationship isn't worth saving or that it's in jeopardy. The problem really lies with what we see, think and feel.

Sure, these are emotions that we are in tune with, but if we're not careful, these emotions can lead us astray if we rely solely on ourselves to problem-solve them. These feelings can be a signal that something is wrong, but without reacting too quickly, what we should do first is pray. Prayer or communicating with God is where we draw our strength from. Prayer is where we get the direction and help we oh-so need in difficult times, as in the relationship of marriage. If both individuals remain committed, if both love and respect one another, there will always be hope.

So how do I begin or how do I pray in the eye of the storm? Philippians 4:6,7 NIRV, **Don't worry about anything. No matter what happens, tell God about everything. Ask and pray and give thanks to Him. (7) Then God's peace will watch over your hearts and your minds.**

The first thing we need to do is simply talk to God and put aside the formalities. God just wants to hear from us. It doesn't matter how you're dressed, what your location is, if you haven't done it before or even if it's been years since you last spoke to Him. God is not keeping score and He definitely isn't out to get you. Contrary to some religions' beliefs, He is a loving God that hears you wherever you are.

How Come My Prayers Haven't Been Answered?

My husband, the good reverend, always tells people that God's answers are: yes, no and not yet. The key to the waiting game is patience, so know that our timing isn't like God's time; a day to Him can literally be a year. 2 Peter 3:8, **A day to the Lord is like a thousand years. And a thousand years is but a day.** I know that sounds horrible in some cases, but know that everything that's happening in your life is working for your benefit, even if it doesn't look like it.

Romans 8:28, **And we know that in all things God works for the good of those who love Him, who have been called according to His purpose.**

How do I know? Well, I was in a 20-year marriage, and for the majority of that time, I prayed for my husband and for things to change. I prayed that he would love me and my children the way we deserved to be loved. I prayed that he would respect me, but unfortunately, that never happened, and things only continued to spiral out of control, and we all ended up enduring abuse. During that time in my life, I expected to hear an audible word from God directing me, guiding me into peace and giving me specific instructions.

Looking back, God definitely was speaking to me, but I didn't pick up on His subtle cues. In retrospect, there were many signs that I either didn't pick up on or was just too afraid to trust Him on. So ultimately, I stayed in the relationship, praying that things would go my way, but in the end, I suffered. I didn't understand at the time, but I had to allow His will to be done in my life and not mine.

Years later, after I finally got the courage to leave, God said, "You didn't trust me." Wow, like a slap in the face, He was right. I thought that I had to be the one to figure it out and come up with the final plans or course of action. But God was showing me all along that the man I was with (my ex-husband) was only going to continue hurting me and my kids, and I needed to save myself and leave.

Of course, I got backlash from this move from so-called Christians saying that I shouldn't divorce, but let me tell you readers something. Never is it okay to be treated with disrespect day after day, year after year. More importantly, when people show you who they are, believe their asses. Through trial and error, I've learned that when God says move, you need to move, **just like that**.

Don't worry about the haters because it is your life and the relationship with the Father that is most important. When you establish a connection with God, He will speak to you and show you things that will simplify and correct the errors in your life. And about divorce, well, if God *never* put the two together, it wasn't His plan in the first place. God doesn't want any of us to suffer and definitely does not want us to be abused. And when infidelity comes into the picture, well, you've just inherited another spirit in your relationship, so something's got to give.

When I look back on all of the challenges and crazy things God put right in front of my face, that I let slide by or ignored, I realized it was Him making it crystal clear that my previous husband didn't love me. Some things were so outlandish it makes me laugh (oh yes, I can laugh at it now, but going through it made me furious) that I didn't make a move sooner, but you have to learn to shake it off. Yes, learn to laugh in the eye of pain instead of focusing on the negativity. Otherwise, it will only keep you down. Looking at Romans 8:28 (the scripture I mentioned above), God was using these various situations to strengthen me and to teach me that I was valuable and worthy of love.

My current husband was also in a similar marriage where he too was cheated on and not given the love he deserved. I remember telling him that I was so happy that God took us through the hurt and pain because we now know how valuable the sanctity of marriage is. We both know the pain that can be rendered when you allow someone to dictate your worth. Our love is so damn amazing, and it is because we both surrendered and were obedient to God that we came to be united.

Now, don't get me wrong, we're not absent of problems; we certainly have had our fair share of obstacles that came our way, but the difference is that we are always willing to handle them together. We take each problem and develop a plan, and we don't let it go until it's completely resolved. We're completely seasoned individuals that can tell you, prayer works! Trusting and waiting on God is the only solution that eradicates any problem.

The other thing that stands out in my previous marriage was that I was trying to turn God's no into my yes. Come on now, how many of us try to help God out or work independently of Him? Whenever He made it clear that he didn't love me, I prayed that God would change him, and I kept trying to be the image of a wife and mother I thought was necessary to make my marriage work.

There's not a chance in heaven for any of us to change the course or the plans that God has for us. Jeremiah 29:11 says, **For I know the plan I have for you declares the Lord, plans to prosper you, not to harm you, plans to give you hope and a future**. Now that's the kind of God I serve! Get in line with the will of God. It is what it is. Accept it and move on because God's plans for our lives are the absolute best.

Chapter 8 - Sex and Things

God Approves of Sex

Having sex, in my experience, has always been this top-secret thing that married couples do. It's something that's not discussed until something foul happens, but an expectation, so to speak, that occurs behind closed doors, almost as if there's something wrong with the experience. Another reason sex isn't discussed in many homes is that it makes some parents feel uncomfortable and/or they just don't know how to broach the subject and end up leaving the subject matter for the schools to discuss. This is totally whack and does not make much sense, since God created man and woman not only to procreate but also for their enjoyment.

Good grief people, sex is a normal part of our development, and it should be discussed in every home so that our young people can make informed choices. The more comfortable we are with our own sexuality and talking about sex with our kids at a level for their ears and understanding, the more we are increasing the odds of them coming to us with the hard stuff and asking for help or more information when they need it.

When referring to intimacy, sex is the most intimate experience or occurrence a couple can have. What comes to mind when I think of sex is its beauty and mysticism. This pleasurable act can literally have you spinning for days and your mind, well, it replays the love and the delightful feelings that came along with it.

All I can say is, God is amazing. He created woman so that man wouldn't be alone; he wanted the two to be united in every possible way, which is why he said in Genesis 2:24 NIV, **That is why a man leaves his father and mother and is united to his wife, and they become one flesh.** Sex or making love is beautiful, it's spiritual and it should be done on a regular basis. It's literally in the word (can't be disobedient) so make it happen.

I Corinthians 7:3 NIV, **The husband should fulfill his marital duty to his wife, and likewise the wife to her husband.**

And the same scripture with the MSG version reads: **It is good for a man to have a wife, and for a woman to have a husband. Sexual drives are strong, but marriage is strong enough to contain them and provide for a balanced and fulfilling sexual life in a world of sexual disorder.**

It can't get any clearer than that!

With all of the chemical changes in the brain that lead to our happy ending, it totally makes sense why we not only enjoy sex (the majority of us, at least) but want more of it when it's over. If you, however, allow too much time to lapse in between making love, the connection diminishes. The love, of course, is still there, as well as the desire to have sex, but the affinity or emotional connection with your partner is decreased. If this is you, I bet your stress levels are climbing through the roof, and if those levels are tame, well, you most definitely took care of it yourself. No shame in the game. Making any sense? Sex is simply hormonal secretions activating mental and bodily changes, but the lack of this means quite the opposite: dead as a doorknob.

So How Much Sex Is a Good Amount to Have?

There's no magic number, so you be the judge and determine what is sufficient for you and your relationship. And talk it over with your partner to see how the two of you can get on the same page; oftentimes there is one person in the relationship that feels they're lacking. For some, a normal sex routine is three times per week, and for others, it could be just once per week.

Just know, the more sex you have, the better your cognition will be, the better you will sleep, your mood will improve, your pain will be more manageable, etc. Seems like a no-brainer to me; the more the merrier, the better you will feel and, in my opinion, you can't have too much.

Also, it is important to note that couples should not keep track of other people's sex lives and performances because everyone's body and situation is quite different. So, what you see on TV is not always an accurate depiction of a true or average sexual relationship. Oh, and for you ladies who are getting up there in age, having more sex equals good vaginal health. Increased blood flow to the genitals during arousal and penetration keeps the tissue from becoming too thin, preventing painful sex and/or irritation, so pick up the pace.

Regularity or consistency is key when discussing sex with your partner. Keep an open dialogue running so as not to make it weird. At the same time, bring a little spontaneity to the party and think outside of the box to keep it interesting. Remember, age is nothing but a number and with age comes wisdom, so get out your trick bags and have fun.

What? No Orgasm?!

When I first heard this, I believe it was on a reality show, and one of the women blurted out, "I've never had an orgasm." I thought, wow, she said that on television. My subsequent thought was how courageous she was for even talking about it for the world to hear. But the reality of the situation is that there are many women across the world that have never had an orgasm and end up faking the funk (not all, but you know who you are).

I want to be your support to find the road that leads to your happy ending. I want for you to be courageous and honest enough to have the conversation about how he (your mate) can help take you there, on that fantastic voyage. In doing my research, and being in deep thought about this topic, I've discovered that women fake orgasms for various reasons. Some just don't find fulfillment in their current sexual relationship and simply want it over with. Then, there are those who can't seem to find the right words to communicate their needs and therefore call it quits, singing "I'm there" when really, they're not. Or perhaps she fakes it because the experience was short-lived, her mate got there first and she doesn't want the spotlight on her. And lastly, we have the other group who have difficulty achieving an orgasm for medical or psychological reasons.

Got to Have it

For those who have never had an orgasm, the newbies (I'm not referring to those with medical issues but the others), we've got some work to do. By definition, according to Dictionary.com, "An orgasm is the physical and emotional sensation experienced at the peak of sexual excitation, usually resulting from stimulation of the sexual organ, and usually accompanied by the male by ejaculation."

Great definition, but we all know that an orgasm can come from any sexual arousal, and this can also come from masturbation or perhaps using sex toys. An orgasm, in my opinion, is like your favorite meal (comfort food) on a sunny day. Wait, I'm not done, it's that warm fuzzy feeling you get when you realize that you're in love for the first time – you know how your heart just throbs.

Nope, not done yet! Couple those emotions with that crazy, fun excitement when you're just about to go down a roller coaster and know that there's no turning back...yowza, yowza, yowza! Ooooh wee, it's good. Now, that's what you call an orgasm, in all of its glory.

So now let's work on getting **you** there. First things first, establish an emotional connection with your partner. What's going on there? Is there any excitement or love transpiring in or out of the bedroom? If you answered "No," Houston, we have a problem.

To enhance your connection with your mate: Love, Listen and Learn. **Love**, not only with words but love your mate with action. Furthermore, never do anything for your partner because you expect something in return; be intentional with your love and let it be the driving force. Then **learn** to actively **listen** to your partner without butting in. I learned this technique in nursing school that totally changed the way I communicate with others. It really works.

Active listening allows for better communication; it's interactive, which means you're not just sitting there like a bump on a log. It involves way more than just opening your ears. With this technique, you're letting that person know that it's all about them. All distractions are eliminated, to the best of your ability, like phones (putting them on silent, off or in another room so that you won't be tempted to pick it up when it illuminates). And if you have children, perhaps you can put the conversation on hold until after they go to bed, allowing you to give your full attention.

Here are the steps you should take to accomplish active listening:

Be All-In – Giving the person your full attention, be mindful to use eye contact. At the same time, use body language that indicates you're invested in the conversation. Try not to fidget, scope out the room, or excessively yawn – all indicators that you are not all-in or not paying attention to what's being said. Facial expressions, on the other hand, should be kept to a minimum, without frowns, winced lips and/or raised eyebrows. And it's okay to let them know you're listening after they've spoken for a couple of minutes, responding with short phrases like okay, yes, uh-huh etc. Moreover, you can let them know you're invested in what they're saying by giving a head nod or two. By giving them signs that you're all-in, you are displaying an element of trust and allowing the other person the freedom and security of being vulnerable, open, honest and confident about conversing in the future.

Give It Back – Try to reiterate the message or statements you've heard and while doing so, ask open-ended questions (these are questions that require more than a yes or no answer) to fully understand your partner's needs.

Almost Done – Now that you have all the necessary information, try and summarize the information, facts and conclusions, giving any needed feedback.

Lastly, to enhance the connection with your partner, you need to learn everything there is to know about them. Typically, when dating individuals, we tend to pick up on the surface stuff, but now that you're in this relationship for the long haul you need to know what makes him or her tick. ☼ Bishop Clark says, "The thing that makes you tick can also be the thing that ticks you off."

Find out about their childhood and connection with family, their parents in particular. Ask questions, get down to the nitty-gritty and find out if they're close, and if not, why? Trust me, it all matters and will most definitely help you connect the dots, understand their personality, behaviors, connections and, most importantly, why you love them.

Equally, ask questions about their friends, even those they don't bring around the house. Find out their aspirations for the next 5-10 years and how they see themselves after retirement. Trust me, you don't want to be surprised. At the same time, you can observe those things that aren't said, like patterns, body language and habits.

All of these things will give you useful information about your partner and assist you in seeing them clearly. Be mindful, though, not to interrogate your partner or aggravate them (they're not in trouble; you're just gathering information). Just converse with the intention of finding out more ways to love them. Explore ways to gather information without it appearing as if you're grilling them. I mean, you are, but perhaps you can do it while giving them a massage or while the two of you are having a quiet moment alone; break it up into segments.

And make it count. Let it be an enjoyable experience for the two of you. Rub his or her temples, give them a foot massage or stroke their necks and tell them how much you adore them. This can be a great time to find out who they really are, and in the end, they will appreciate you for taking the time to know them on a deeper level.

In the first few years of our relationship, I used to ask about my husband's mother, and he would always shut me down. She's been deceased for a number of years (20+), but it was always a touchy subject. Furthermore, he never had any pictures of her around and didn't want any put on the walls (I'm a picture person. I love them, so much so that there aren't many free spaces on our walls).

Around the holidays, he would give me nuggets and divulge how much he enjoyed Thanksgiving because he and his mother would cook together; he would be her sous-chef. After probing time and time again (I would occasionally find him sulking a few days out of the year), he finally broke down and told me that he missed her terribly and talking about her made him unhappy.

Not leaving it there, I countered with, "Yes. but talking about her allows me to know her, and I want to know the mother you loved." Later, I found a picture and blew it up, put it on the living room wall (as a surprise) and boy, was he happy. Even though talking about his mother was a sore subject, I believe the communication allowed much-needed healing to take place. Adding her to the mix, in my opinion, decreased the episodes of extreme sadness he felt, especially around her birthday and the events surrounding her death. Learning about my mother-in-law helped me to connect on a deeper level with my husband. So, learn all you can about your mate; it will strengthen your love.

Now, it's time to work on *you*. It's time to see if there is anything in your past that is preventing you from connecting on an emotional level. Could there be a past hurt that was never resolved? A form of abuse that you are unintentionally carrying around on a daily basis? A hurt you thought you dealt with, but now, here we go again, the hurt is bubbling up, causing harm and stealing your joy?

Sometimes we carry around baggage with a completely different label on it. We think it's anger because someone cut into our lane while driving, they looked at us the wrong way in the grocery store or possibly said something negative, and we labeled our reaction "anger." But what it really is, deep down inside, is us responding in fury because we don't have **peace over our past**: peace over past hurts that were never discussed and thus, we end up lashing out over small things, things that we otherwise should have let go of.

Similarly, have you truly learned how to love and be emotionally tied to another human being? There are so many adults that were never shown love, i.e., never hugged as kids, never given the necessary attention, never told they were loved or possibly there was no image of love shown or displayed in the home, for whatever reason.

When you are genuinely loved, and that love was or is put on display for you, you're able to give love more freely. A perfect example of this is the love God displays towards us every single day, waking us up and providing for us when we do not deserve it. That's Grace. And how about sending His son to die on the cross for our sins? Now, you know we didn't deserve that one either.

So, what am I saying? If you don't have the capacity to show or provide love, perhaps it may be a good idea to talk it over with a therapist. Take the necessary steps to clean out your emotional closets so that your relationship will have a fighting chance.

Just in Case You Forgot, We're Still Discussing Orgasms!

Next, take any pressure off yourself that may be there from previous experiences or relationships. If you are giving yourself a hard time for not being able to experience an orgasm, stop and know that it is okay. Slowly but surely, let it go because that added pressure is hindering your ability to experience pure bliss. There are millions of people who have been where you are right now.

So, if you're able to *stop* focusing on having an orgasm and simply enjoy your emotional and physical connection with your mate, knowing that things will soon be changing, you're getting somewhere. Because where there's passion, the feeling is bound to come, or cum, if you give it time.

I said this previously, but I'll say it again. If you know your body and what makes you feel good, it is highly probable that you can experience an orgasm. To take it a step further, try and experience every sensation your body has to offer (and there are many). Practice with your hand or a vibrator (yes, a vibrator). The end goal here is to share this with your partner.

Be okay with telling yourself that it feels good. Of course it does, God made us all sexual beings and He gave us every last hormone and chemical in the body to allow us these feelings. And moan, for goodness' sake. Let out that sexual tension; trust and believe that it will help take you there.

To go deeper, when you moan for your partner, it's letting him or her know that you're turned all the way on and that they've hit the right spot. My husband says that it actually turns him on when I moan or talk to him during our sexual experiences, so don't hesitate to give it a shot. Trust me, I was shy at first, but now there is absolutely no hesitation on my part.

Once you learn your own body, you can teach him or her how you did it with a game of Simon says. Try, "Simon says gently stroke my clitoris and don't stop until I purr," or say, "Simon says, stop." Make it fun and don't hold anything back; you can even turn your body into a human boardwalk and allow your partner to travel across you, allowing him or her to score points along the way for making you squeal. Whatever works – there are no wrong ways to pleasure each other, unless however, one of you disagrees.

After a few demonstrations, you will be hot and ready for intercourse, using every little trick and tip you've learned along the way, paying close attention to applying pressure on the clitoris and making pit stops to those erogenous zones. *See the erogenous zones diagram for clarity.

Don't Fake the Funk

I've heard of women faking this experience, although I'm not too sure why because you want your partner to know that he hit that good ole' spot. Ladies, I don't know if this is you, but there may be times when you may be tired or possibly want to stroke his ego during love-making, but being dishonest in this area is not the best solution. Chances are if he didn't help you achieve the touchdown, he'll run that play again (or won't do what it takes for you to climax) and this will only lead to frustration on your part. As the famous line from The Color Purple says, "Don't do it, Ms. Celie."

So, what do you do when you're not in the mood? Communicate it! And give an alternate solution to not being in the mood, like tomorrow, or later that evening; give him or her something tangible to go by. Also, give them an explanation, telling him or her why you're not in the mood. Are you sick (I mean, really sick), or maybe you're stressed or distracted, with a lot on your mind, etc.?

The best medicine is honesty in this situation. But know that sex is one of the links in marriage that keeps the connection or bond intact. I didn't say the only thing, but you have to admit it's essential. You want your partner to feel wanted in this way, so giving him or her reassurance is key.

Perhaps you are in the mood, and it's finally happening, but your partner is closer to an orgasm than you. What do you do? Do you just go along with the flow and pretend you're there too? Nope! When my husband is near his breaking point, and I can literally feel his rocket getting ready to launch, but I'm not quite there – stop! Switch gears and tell him you're not ready. Change positions, anything to stop the rhythmic flow.

Here's the wonderful thing about our relationship: because we're so connected, he definitely wants to take me there, so he will more than likely comply with my request. Now, there have been times when he just says, "Sorry, babe," and I just let him enjoy his win. At no time do I do a moan-along, giving him the impression of victory. I'm not setting myself up to be robbed of this glory, no, sir. So, if I don't achieve an orgasm, nine times out of ten, we keep going until I do. But if that doesn't happen, if the party is really over and there's no more boom for me, he'll offer to perform oral sex. You see, when you stay in the honest seat, you can still reach glory. And Let the Church say, *Amen!*

Don't Stop!

Ladies, what do you do when you know it's about *that* time, and you're not there yet? If your response is, "Nothing!" that would be the wrong response. First, I would highly advise you to familiarize yourself with the actual signs or to pick up on the visual cues and know what it feels like when he is getting ready to inoculate you with his love. I would be remiss if I didn't mention that there are times when he says he's coming, and he is actually a long way off. When my husband says "Almost, babe," it may easily be another 10-15 minutes.

You see, he's a preacher. If any of you are not familiar, when a Baptist minister/preacher says he's ending or concluding, it means nada. In my mind, he's telling me that he is wrapping things up, that it's coming to a close, that he is getting ready to cum and be done. But he literally has the propensity to keep things going for as long as he likes (I'd like to take this time and say, "Thank You, Lord!").

Anyway, when my husband uses those words, and I miss the visual signs or feelings, I immediately put him on high alert and tell myself to stop procrastinating and get mine. I so, enjoy the feeling of how he puts it on me, so I'm literally basking in his love at that point.

On the other hand, if his face takes a sudden shift from bliss to "yikes," it's about to go down. It's at that time that I can actually feel his penis growing and pulsating. Ladies, when you're at this point and feel that explosion coming your way and you're not yet ready yourself, you can do these things:

The first and most obvious thing to do is pull away and just say, "Nope, not yet." Don't forget to look at the expression on his face when you make this move because he will not be a happy camper. Take charge at this point; it's a buffet and he can literally get (or eat) all he wants. He just has to come back to the table.

Next, when you feel that pulsation and growth, perform a Kegel or two and hold it for a couple of seconds. That light squeeze will slow down the blood supply to the penis and oh, watch his face! When I clamp down on my husband's love stick, his whole body tenses up and his eyes become scrunched, and then he says, "Come on, babe." It is some funny stuff, but it works. If, by chance, you can't pull it off, perhaps because your muscles aren't as strong as you would like them to be at this point, pull away and take that penis all the way out.

So, if you haven't experienced that feeling or been able to pick up on cues just yet, try to pay close attention to his body language and possibly his unintelligible words. But if he tells you it's almost over, gives you a weak apology, or you see that look on his face (that says the rocket is about to launch), you can also try this: take your fingers, while he's still inside of you, and give his penis a nice finger hug (squeeze it). Again, it will slow down the blood flow, slowing down the ejaculation process.

Lastly, to slow down the process, just tell him to stop. My husband and I have been at this junction many times, and we've coined it our time-out period. Here, we just stop all motion, look into each other's eyes, and talk. If you can't do it, pull away! When we call a break-time, after approximately 15 seconds, one of us happens to start our love motions again, but at least it slows things down for a moment. Again, just learn to have fun and laugh because life is way too short.

What Is Orgasmic Dysfunction?

Now, this refers to situations where women aren't able to achieve a climax on their own. It can happen in men as well, but this is more common in women. I remember a time when my husband was rubbing the hell out of my clitoris and nothing was happening, I mean no wet stream, no excitation, nada. I couldn't figure it out because this had never happened to me before. I attributed it to menopause, but I still wasn't sold on that being the culprit.

Finally, it clicked when I remembered my doctor had written me a prescription for an anti-depressant as a way to deal with my fibromyalgia. This just happened to be the culprit. The medication ended up causing major gastric problems, so I eventually stopped taking it. And this was my ticket to waterworks again.

My story is one that is quite common as to the reasons for not being able to have an orgasm: it is a side-effect of some medications. At the same time, because of my crazy body, *pain* is another problem that at times prevents me from the final score.

If pain is a part of your daily life, as it is mine, it is important to pre-medicate so that you can have an enjoyable experience. Now, speaking of pain medication, I will take half the dose before and the other half after because it will totally ruin the experience by taking the complete dose. This is my experience, so talk to your doctor before making any changes with your medication.

I also know that the sexual experience will release various hormones that work in assisting with pain relief. Pain medication can also cause a delay in or can inhibit an orgasm, so again, talk to your doctor about this problem if this happens to be you so the two of you can put together a regime that works for you.

Here is a list of some categories of medication that can lead to sexual dysfunction:

- Pain medication
- Diabetes medication
- Cholesterol medications
- Anti-depressants
- Anti-anxiety medications

If you are experiencing sexual dysfunction relating to your medication, even those that I haven't included in this section, talk to your doctor because there may be another medication in the same class that won't affect your system in this way.

Hold It!

Women have been told time and time again to perform Kegel exercises after birth to strengthen their pelvic floor muscles, which can become weak during pregnancy and childbirth. These muscles can also become weak as we age, if you've had certain pelvic surgeries, have chronic constipation or even obesity. And for men, these muscles can become weak with prostate surgery.

If you're not too sure if you have this problem, you may know these muscles are weak if you're in a hurry to urinate and just can't seem to make it to the bathroom in time. Or perhaps you leak when you cough or sneeze, or even more unsettling, have a little "poopsy" in your pants when either of the two are happening. Men, too, can have these same problems, perhaps resulting from diabetes, prostate surgery, or an overactive bladder. Kegels work for them as well.

So, if you're thinking, what do Kegels have to do with this book? Well, the answer is to improve your overall quality of life, and of course, to improve sexual function. And since we were just talking about orgasms, they help with those too, according to Dr. Ruth and Time.com. Yes! Kegels help build strong muscles down there, thereby heightening the overall sexual experience. And according to Women's Health, performing Kegels can not only heighten the sensations but will increase orgasmic chances. So, who's with me in learning more?

Kegels are simple to do, they don't cost a thing and they can be done without anyone else knowing – easy peasy. For those of you who don't know what the heck I'm talking about, Kegels are exercises performed to strengthen the muscles surrounding our bladder, bowels and uterus (in women). The muscles used for these purposes are consequently the same muscles used when we climax. See where I'm going with this? These muscles are not only useful, but they're also essential.

When these muscles are in optimal shape, they lead to more enjoyable sex because the intensity is catapulted – **yes**! This improves our sexual arousal by way of increasing the blood circulation to the pelvic floor. And where there's increased blood flow, there's a stronger erection, which means a harder penis, and we all love a harder penis, right?

At the same time, in women, Kegels help with increased natural lubrication, and this is a good thing if you want to keep things going and pleasurable at the same time. For men, this means that during sexual intercourse, there is a stronger chance that the penis will remain hard longer, by way of stronger surrounding muscles.

Furthermore, by doing Kegels, men will be able to control and hold off an ejaculation a wee bit longer. Now, that sounds like a win to me. Likewise, performing Kegels and thereby attaining a stronger pelvic floor muscle can assist with urinary incontinence in both men and women. I don't know about you, but if performing Kegels helps with orgasms and increased sensation during sex, I'll do them in my sleep.

So, now let's talk about how to locate and perform Kegels. To find out which muscle I'm referring to, if you've ever been in a hurry to urinate but couldn't find a bathroom, that tightening and pain you feel between your legs, that's the muscle. If you find that you're unable to isolate or find this muscle, hold your urine stream the next time you're in the bathroom. Bingo! Once you've found the correct muscle, you can begin strengthening it.

Don't practice this exercise while urinating (only to locate the muscle) as it can cause irritation to the bladder and damage to the muscle. Talk to your medical provider if you still need further assistance and direction.

Steps to take:

1. Relax! To start, try lying down and releasing any tension you may have. Don't tense any muscle in your body.

2. Now, contract the pelvic floor for five seconds and release for the same amount of time; hold for five seconds, release for five seconds. Sometimes it can be hard for some people to locate the muscle. So, women,

you can try inserting a finger into the vagina and then tightening the surrounding muscles without tightening or contracting your abdomen, buttocks, or legs.

You can also use a vibrator and use the same technique. For fun, I like to use my husband's penis in the spur of the moment; really, it's just to see his facial expression. Give it a try and practice this technique. Don't worry, it won't hurt, but he will feel it and may even find it enjoyable.

Men, you can also locate the muscle by interrupting the flow of urine. Once found, hold the muscle for five seconds and release for the same amount of time If you're still not able to find the correct muscle, you can also pretend that you're holding in your gas or poop; if you can do that, you are working the right muscle.

My husband likes to show off his hard penis by having it jump up and down or wave at me. Yep! Same muscle. Whatever works for you and in turn strengthens your pelvic floor muscle, do it! What's most important is that you do it.

Once you have this exercise down, you can begin to increase the duration and frequency, holding the muscle for five seconds, performing it up to 10 times twice per day. It can be done before getting out of bed, in the shower, in the grocery store, or while driving to work. As long as you are isolating the muscle without the use of the abdomen, buttocks, and thighs you are on your way to a more intense sexual experience. You'll thank me for this. You're welcome!

Chapter 9 – *The Big Comeback*

———————⟡⟡⟡———————

Failure Is Not a Permanent Condition!

When we think of the word failure, we often think of not being good enough or being less than, but this is far from the truth. While the word failure implies that we are deficient in an area, when I think of this word, I think, "comeback." Whatever area in your life you may fall short in, begin to see your way out of that place and envision yourself having no lack.

Don't allow your frustrations to speak failure; trust God and know that there is hope for any situation you may face. Things can turn around. Whatever that thing is in your life that is bringing you down, could it be something that can make you and/or your situation better in time? Or, if the deficit is something that you can't change, are you able to look at it with a different perspective or new set of lenses, thereby improving your overall mental health?

When I think of my situation, it's hard not to stay fixated on the constant pain and looming exhaustion I face every single day. Not long ago, I could only focus on the negativity and problems because they overwhelmingly consumed me. As a nurse, I quickly realized that I was in a state of depression and just that fact alone infuriated me. I could not see a way out because my symptoms were there every second of the day. Moreover, I didn't understand why God would allow me to suffer in this way; I mean, didn't He love me? I knew in my heart that He did, but I sure didn't feel it at the time.

You see, I was a nurse who couldn't function in that role any longer, and it pissed me off. Equally, I was a wife and mother (of a combined eight kids) with two small children in the home, and I could no longer live up to my role of either. What in the hell was going on? The bigger question was, why?

My husband and family helped me in every possible way: literally helping me in and out of the shower and washing my body when I couldn't, taking the kids (off and on) so they didn't have to see me in that way. My family was standing in the gap for me in prayer when I couldn't do it myself. My family is a Godsend. The thought of life being over gave me solace, yet again, it angered me, even being comfortable with the idea of not being here any longer. I could not imagine the coming days being like the previous ones. What was I to do?

I remember a dear friend who I hadn't spoken with in many years calling to check in, and me giving her a rundown on my condition. My takeaway from our conversation was hearing that her mother had suffered from a similar condition but improved (this is one of those "but God" moments). This gave me comfort and was my first glimmer of hope.

I used to lay in bed crying all the time; nothing brought me joy. There was nothing positive about life that I could point out. It felt as if I were dying. Well, I didn't know what was causing my decline in health, especially in the first two years when the doctors couldn't give me any answers at all but continued to prescribe different medications to control my symptoms. Life was bad; I mean, no light anywhere to be found.

When things are spiraling out of control in life, look for that safety net, rely on God and know that He loves and wants the absolute best for you, even if you cannot see it.

My husband and family prayed daily, and something finally clicked, and I was able to pray for myself. I finally realized that God was taking care of me and I had nothing to do with it. You see, before the illness, I relied on Me. I had a good job making great money, and my husband and I were making it happen. Even though I went to church every Sunday, was a Sunday school teacher and directed the kids' choir and dance group with my sister, I never knew God was in control of my being.

Even though I was all-in, or so I thought, God wasn't first, I was. Yes, I prayed, but I didn't consult God before I took action. I never waited for His answer; I didn't have a rooted relationship with Him, so He had to get my attention.

As I lay in my bed, weak and not able to do much of anything, I was able to clearly see that God was providing all of our needs. I truly lived Philippians 4:19, **And my God shall supply all your needs according to His riches in Christ Jesus**. I read that scripture before and totally believed in God and what He could do, but never had I *lived it*. I had no job, was denied any long-term insurance, couldn't physically take care of my kids or myself or be a wife to my husband. And as I mentioned before, my husband had a work injury that almost cost him his life, and he had to retire early. God took the lead, literally. He took care of everything. He is so amazing.

So, when things look grim, don't think for a second that you're counted out of the race or that there is no other option. When you have downtime, take a break and recharge your mind and body. Don't keep your head down; try to find something positive about your life or your current situation.

Philippians 4:8 tells us **to think about what's true, whatever is pure, whatever is lovely, what is admirable, if anything is excellent or praiseworthy, think about such things.**

In other words, find whatever glimmer of light or hope you can and focus on that. Whether it's our parents' presence or the fact that our parents gave us life, being thankful for our children, the activities of our limbs, the sky, moon, the flowers, whatever. If we continue to focus on the good around us, whatever that is, and praise God for those things each day, things will get better – at least our mental status will (He'll put things into perspective), and that's the most important part if you ask me. So, when things are chaotic and you don't know which way to turn, look up!

When the majority of my issues began, my husband would always say, "Pray, babe." My husband is always right by my side to guide me, and he's also my sounding board. When things got too difficult for me, he would grab me by my hand and just start praying, as would my family. We all need a spiritual partner who supports us. One who will pray without asking for the details, someone who will remain neutral and hold your hand through the storms of life. If you don't have one, get one. You can also be the one to develop that bond or relationship with someone else. God will lead you through it.

Do You Find Yourself Desirable?

If you don't have the self-confidence you desire, could this be the reason things aren't hot and steamy in the bedroom? I've often been in the habit of self-criticism, or I put myself down, per my husband, and have a hard time receiving compliments. I guess I never really saw myself as pretty or good enough, especially after the difficulty in my first marriage. I remember not being able to look at myself in the mirror because of how my ex-husband made me feel. I really had some issues and ultimately wasn't strong enough to see myself for who I was.

When you allow others to put you down, or if you keep taking the shit they throw, not to mention not knowing your worth, this can have a crippling effect on your psyche. This can eventually spill over into the lives of those you're in close proximity with. For me, it was my kids. I'm just so thankful that those days are far behind me and that I have a man who loves me. He loves me unconditionally, and he doesn't hold my deficiencies against me, but neither do I. Did I mention earlier that God hooked us up?

It's my prayer that you know without a shadow of a doubt that you are beautiful, that you are worthy and that you were designed to love and be loved. Psalms 139:14 says, **we are fearfully and wonderfully made by God.** Translation, God is a Bad Man (or Spirit, correctly put) and since we're made in his image, we are better than good enough, we are phenomenal, we are worthy, a prize catch.

Take some time for you, getting to know what tickles your fancy. Take the time to repair any negative self-images you may have drawn for yourself or that you've allowed others to paint of you. Tear down any walls of pain, frustration, or any body image disorder that you may be carrying around; just kick that extra baggage to the curb.

Turn it around and learn to love the image that you see in the mirror, and if by chance you don't like what you see, change it. Change the things you can and pray for the wisdom and peace to accept those you can't. God crafted you in his infinite wisdom, and at the end of the day, He said it was all good.

So, if God sees you as a precious gem, then it is so. What will also give you an edge is if you write words of affirmation around the house. Write them on post-its (sticky notes) on the bathroom wall, on the mirrors you frequent and even tape them on your computer screens. Whatever you need to do to remember, do that.

If you need ideas, write:

- I am Beautiful
- I am Powerful
- I am Victorious
- I can do all things through Christ who gives me strength
- I am Valuable
- I am Worthy of Love
- I am Blessed
- I am more than a Conqueror
- Greater is He that's in me than he that's in the world
- ☀ No weapon formed against me shall prosper

Get my drift? If these don't work for you, take the time to create your own powerful, life-changing words. What's most important is that you begin self-care and learn to repair any damage that may have taken place in your past. Know without a shadow of a doubt that you are a winner, a beautiful work of art and a prize to be had.

So, now that you know that you're all that and so much more, act like it. Flip the switch, walk with your head held high, put some attitude in your step and walk like you know you're the bomb because you are. The time is now to create positive, lasting, loving memories with your mate, those you both will never forget.

It took a bit of time to accept me, but I had the help of my husband who literally nursed me back to health (the preacher helping the nurse). He helped me to realize my worth, my value in life and that I was beautiful, something I never saw myself as. The more you tell yourself that you're worthy and beautiful, the clearer a picture will ensue and the easier you will see yourself in the frame. It will be as if you got cataracts removed from your eyes: at first, the image was distorted, blurry and unable to show the fine details of life.

But oh, the transformation when the build-up or decay is removed from the naked eye, it will be like night and day. The image is up close and so deeply personal; you can then see what God has been seeing all along. And when you finally realize what was there, you will rise to the occasion and step into your rightful role and meet it with confidence.

Marijuana

I thought this section was necessary because there are some individuals, well, I'll just come out and say it, you church folks that need to know that it's okay to use marijuana, weed, the purple or whatever you call it, to control your symptoms (you name it). As a nurse, I've always believed or understood that there was a medical need for marijuana (for others, not just for myself). MJ/weed/THC therefore has its place when it comes to pain control, loss of appetite, anxiety disorders, suppressing the effects of epilepsy, managing side-effects from cancer, PTSD, and the list goes on.

As I gaze over my life, I've been able to see the transition, not to mention the bad rap marijuana has received in previous years as being one used only by the lower socioeconomic class or those on the other side of the track, so to speak. But we all know this is a misnomer, it couldn't be further from the truth. Need I remind you of our unnamed president's use and the controversy, not to mention the comedy, surrounding it to this day?

Well, the negative backlash and/or rhetoric, in my opinion, was because of the many images displayed on television and film of what individuals could become, bottom feeders so to speak, if they consumed Mary Jane. Hmm, what about now? With the legalization (in certain states) and shops popping up all across the world, more and more individuals have come out of the closet and not just for medical reasons, people love this stuff.

In current times, many of us have seen MJ become the new Tylenol, sold everywhere and coming soon to a pop-up shop near you. Marijuana is normalized now, and why? Is it because of the all-mighty dollar (cha-ching)? Well, that is apparently ringing true, even in Congress, but the effects, yes, the effects of marijuana in its natural state are still the same. The new strains, however, are of course more potent, but the view today is one of consent, pleasure, and the drug is looked at as being all good.

I can honestly say that my view of marijuana in previous days was also a negative one (aside from medical use) because of my experience as a child being asked by a friend's parent in 5th grade if I wanted to smoke some as he passed a joint to his niece. Really? Grown-ass man! Trying to introduce marijuana to a child, and one he'd never met before? Even though I had never been exposed, I knew it wasn't a cigarette because of the smell; my father smoked cigarettes, and I instantly knew that it was wrong, so I got out of there quickly and ran home. Forging ahead as a young adult and holding on to the mixed bag of truths, I had to get to a place of understanding and see what value marijuana had, if any.

I'll say it again: but what about today? The increased use with adolescents, especially now that it's legal in many parts, not to mention the convenience in disguising it, has continued to soar, but what about the effects on their brains? What people (young adults or individuals in general) don't take into consideration is that brain development is not complete until the mid-20s, so drug intake or use can have horrendous effects like difficulty maintaining focus and attention, difficulty with concentration/thinking, memory deficits, poor academic performance, impaired drive, not to mention the risk of altering the compositions of the brain, according to a study by the National Institute of Health and the Mayo Clinic.

The takeaway here is that adolescents should be using this valuable time to soak up life, not to mention their education, without their brains being put on hold or altered with a substance put in their bodies. Moreover, if a person isn't mature enough to control themselves and know when to stop, it can change their focus and for some, it will be a gateway to other drugs.

Parenting tip: Stop allowing your kids to frequent every friend's home, or even family members' for that matter, until you are 100% positive that the adults in the home won't negatively affect your child to the point of no return. Family are those you are connected with by blood, but it in no way means they will have the same values as you, so protect your kids at all costs.

So, what was the change for me in how I viewed MJ for personal use? It was that *crazy pain* and much coaxing from my husband and son. As time progressed, I eventually started having gastric problems (from the various medications trying to manage my symptoms) and in the process, lost a total of 20 lbs. because of the long-term use of certain medications coupled with the stress of my condition. It ended up being a breeding ground for disaster in my gut, making food my enemy.

A doctor recommended marijuana's use, so I got a medical card years ago to help with my overall pain, but after trying different products, I didn't find MJ completely effective. I tried creams, tinctures, candy and even the vape pen. It was somewhat helpful for my insomnia and migraines but for my back and hip pain, not in the least bit. I also noticed that it helped with my overall mood that had taken a dive with the decline in my health and, much to my surprise, it helped with sexual arousal.

Yes, you read that correctly, sexual arousal. Now, I guess the inclusion of this topic is making sense. Sex is the greatest activity since sliced bread, thank you, Lord! And during my trial or experimental phase, I noticed that my body was relaxed. It took the intensity off certain pain, not to mention the tension that pain can bring, and allowed me to be in a place of "I'm ready!" Yes, I'm still talking about sex. I wanted my husband, and I mean with an urgency, and he surely didn't mind it, not at all. And the act of making love seemed to go on and on, being something I will always remember; no fluff there.

Not only was I aroused, but it heightened the entire climactic experience. I was ready to shout, "Hallelujah!" I mean a completely mind-blowing encounter. In my opinion, what made it all the more satisfying was the fact that I wasn't expecting it and had never heard of this effect before. I mean, wow! Okay, so I'm definitely not pushing MJ, but if you have it in your possession and are using it anyway, it's at least worth a try. Especially if you're like me, willing to try anything to get your pain under control that, consequently, won't damage your kidneys or liver. Okay, I'll get off the subject of sex for now, but just for a moment.

Managing pain can be tricky and downright overwhelming. You sometimes have to try a gazillion products before you find that one needle in a haystack or elixir that works for you. For me, what it boiled down to was comfort, so despite my previous views, I was willing to try it and mark it off the list of things that I tried but didn't work. If you are going this route, get a journal and document your experience. Make a notation of what you took and how it made you feel, not to mention how long you had to wait to get the desired effects.

You can also find comfort in knowing that many doctors recommend MJ's use because of its benefits and effectiveness shown through clinical trials with many people afflicted and experiencing an array of symptoms. Please discuss it with your physician before jumping on the bandwagon because although it may be the product that takes the intensity off whatever symptom you're facing, it can also have untoward effects when dealing with different medical conditions, like heart disease.

The long and short of it, during my experimental period, was determining that THC wasn't for me. While I had some positive experiences during my trial, I also noticed that with some forms, I had feelings of increased anxiety, increased heart rate, difficulty sleeping and paranoia. No thank you, ma'am! It's important to note that not everyone will have the same effects; some are more sensitive to these products than others, so puff with caution. And as for me, I'll just stick with my CBD creams to keep it safe.

Overall, the problem with this drug is that it can have damaging effects on the body with extended use. Of course, this is something that is not talked about, at least I'd never heard of its specifics. The trouble with marijuana is not only its stupor-like side-effects or some individuals not being motivated to work hard or be their best, but that this drug can change the course of lives if not used carefully.

Some things people may notice are: increased appetite (totally not good for those who are obese), stimulated senses and altered thought processes (sight, sound, time and touch). Mary Jane impairs the ability to problem solve, to think coherently; it can increase anxiety (not in every person; for some MJ helps with anxiety disorders). You can experience panic attacks, psychosis (delusions, hallucinations), lung problems, low testosterone (that's right! So, if you're having trouble getting it up, this may be the reason) and heart damage. These are definitely things that many individuals experience when using TCH. Some of these side effects are mild, but others can be deadly. So, I'll say it one last time: **puff with caution**.

I asked my son-in law and fitness expert, Glyndelle Poole to comment on this topic.

When asked to chime in on this topic, I would say that physical pain lead this subject to MJ's use, as well as the recreational aspects. Many people use it to cope with emotional damage, post-trauma and to escape the chaotic realities of this world. As for me, it was all the above. I noticed that it was a lot easier to spark up a joint instead of facing the pain of my childhood and shortcomings.

But, when that joint was lit, my perception changed; the intensity of those negative thoughts and the emotions that came along with them would fade away. The high would eventually fade away but the issues, those things that haunted me, remained unchanged. The reality was that I needed to face my fears and change my perspective, instead of running to a joint when things got tough.

In the end, the fact that I smoked and abused the action made me feel unworthy to go out and pursue the things that God had placed in me long before I was introduced.

My position is not that consumption of weed is bad, just bad for me. In this season of my life, I need focus, fuel and confidence, instead of being high. For some, they may be able to indulge and still make life happen, but for me, it started to become a hindrance.

In my opinion, for those who haven't tried it or are just starting out, it would be wise for you to ponder honestly if it is a need for you. If not, you should find a healthier hobby. (G. Poole Fit4Life Co.)

What Gets You in the Mood?

When the topic of making love comes up, there are couples who can jump right in with just the mere word, sex, while others may need a little extra time warming up to the idea.

For me, it's the thought or recollection of feelings from the last escapade. The sheer thought of his hands on my body, and don't get me started with the feelings that linger when he touches the honey pot, oh, Lord! As for my husband, well, he's ready any morning (he's horny in the morning, y'all) of any day of the week. And if he happens to pull up our photos or videos from his phone, well, he will be ready **any** time of the day or night.

Aside from this, creating an atmosphere of fun and pleasure can help to create a mood of love-making. Even though we're all different, there are some things you can do to kick things into high gear.

The other night after the kids were down, my husband finally decided to give me a full body massage. I don't know what I did to deserve it, but I'm so glad he did. He first came and asked what kind of oil I wanted him to use, lotion, coconut oil or shea butter. Since I suffer from chronic back pain, he then asked if I wanted him to use any of the arthritis creams I had. That would be a, "Yeah-no!"

I mean, yes, it was a wonderful idea that would have taken the edge off my pain, but I was totally trying to get some, and I didn't want our sense of smell to take the fun off the table. This was a time for oral medication to assist with my pain control. It's important to note that my husband did not have sex on his radar (go figure!). So, this was a time for me to use temptation as a way to put him in the right frame of mind, so I seductively pulled my panties down under my derriere and then waited for the effects.

Anyway, back to the oil. Our go-to is always coconut oil for anything related to the skin and hair, so he came into the room prepared to pamper me. I also thought it would be the perfect time to try this new CBD cream my daughter bought me, so here we go.

Touch is so very important, not to mention vital to any relationship. Touch nurtures, it heals, and it ignites intimacy to the next level. When my husband usually gives me a rub down, it's typically with one hand, his left, dominant hand, and it usually ends after five measly minutes with him saying, "Babe, my hand hurts," but not this time. It was as if Gomer Pyle was shouting on a loudspeaker, "Surprise, surprise, surprise!" I felt as if it were my birthday or something.

I don't know what brought this idea of a massage on; was it that no kids were scurrying around? Did it have anything to do with the dim lights and the slow R&B music playing in the background? Or was it the visual of my "Vickies" that day. Well, now he had a amazing visual of my bare butt in his face, not to mention nothing else on? I was just lying there like a pretty, delicate flower, ready to be picked.

Well, whatever it was, this massage went on forever it seemed. When it rolled past the one-hour mark, I wanted to pay him (not in money of course, but you know, in services). I mean, really, it was one of the best massages I've ever had, and he used both hands, look at God! This is what tipped the cards in my favor. Ladies, ask for what you want. I asked, "Babe, is this leading to something?" His astounding response was, "It can if you want it to." Good glory of God!

I mean, he did gingerly stroke my labia a few times – hmm, was that accidental? I don't know. Well, maybe the first time, but it happened again. I'm sure he knew what he was doing with those light yet firm strokes of his hands, all the while sending me into a spiral of ecstasy.

So, what am I saying? A massage before sex is one of the absolute best foreplay methods a couple can use. I'd even go as far to say that it's essential. Having a massage, or the two performing a massage on each other, is beneficial to get you all wet and bothered, not to mention what's needed to prompt you for an orgasm. Bingo!

Getting back to my husband, his lips didn't really move at all during the massage, he just let his hands do the talking with just the right amount of pressure, before using his mouthpiece (now you can take that any way you'd like). He went all-in and didn't leave any body part untouched. He was touching my internal senses without even knowing it. Remember the diagram of the different erogenous zones? Well, Mr. Washington stroked my neck, my back and legs with his hot lubricated hands. And when he touched my vagina, Jesus Christ! I was ready, which brings me to the next section, lubricants.

Lubricants

For many years, KY Jelly and Vaseline have been the mainstays for assisting women with vaginal dryness. There are those who don't require any assistance at all, while others require it more frequently. If your vagina gets dry from time to time, know that it is perfectly normal, especially if you guys are kicking it into overtime (the more sex the better).

First off, ladies, don't hesitate to tell your partner that you *both* need some assistance with lubrication because it will not only be less painful (a dry vagina during sex can cause damage to the lining, causing tears, bleeding and infection) but it will be a more enjoyable experience if you apply some lube. For this section, I made some adjustments to a few of the stanzas from the song "Slide Some Oil to Me" by Charlie Smalls, from The Wiz. If you remember it, sing it to your man, but if you've never heard it before, pop over to YouTube and play it while you add the changes below (it's not the full song).

Slide some oil to me

Let it trickle down my spot

If you don't have any K.Y.J.

Coconut will do just fine

Slide some to my thighs

And to my vagina, if you would

Slide some oil to me man

Whooo, yes that feels good

Slide some oil to my breast

Look a there, I've got a spark again, come on

Slide some oil to my spot

And let me see you slide in

Slide some oil to me

I'm beginning to feel alive

Slide some oil to me babe

And let me lubricate inside

I don't know what made me think of this song, but it surely fits.

Chapter 10 – *What Can I Do?*

There are quite a few products on the market (over-the-counter products) to relieve vaginal dryness, as well as those that can be prescribed by your doctor or gynecologist. With the various options out there, many people end up with an array of products just sitting in their bathroom cabinets or on their bedside tables after exploring and figuring out if they liked them or not.

I've tried a few products over the years, but I never liked the tackiness, the smell or the taste associated with them. In my experience, it ends up being a total waste of money, when all you really need to do is head to your kitchen cabinets for the answer. My husband and I use coconut oil whenever we need a little "umph" to keep things going, or sliding, shall I say.

Yes, coconut oil because it's natural, it smells good, and most people have it in their kitchens. It is an excellent solution for dry, chapped skin. We use it as an after-shower lubricant as well as for our son who has eczema; it calms the skin down due to its anti-inflammatory and anti-bacterial properties. Coconut oil is also good as an additive in baked goods, salad dressings, oil for sautés and main dishes. I also love using this oil as a make-up remover. If you've never tried it, it totally removes everything gently; simply wash your face afterwards and it leaves your skin moisturized and smooth.

You can also use coconut oil as a base for body scrubs, leaving the skin supple. There are so many uses for this wonder oil, so why not use it sparingly to moisten the outer labia? Don't knock it until you've tried it. Other natural oils you can try are aloe (pure) or avocado oil. Just think about it, feeling his hot, lubricated hands all over your body, slipping into your crevices would be amazing. Couples! Ladies! Get some natural oils in your homes to enhance your sexual experience; you won't regret it.

Some Possible Problems Associated with Vaginal Dryness

I must admit that I like a little friction with entry from time to time, but too much can cause damage to my delicate flower. When women have problems with moisture in the vaginal canal, it can be due to any number of things, but let's explore some possible causes.

Not enough foreplay or lack thereof – When we are aroused enough, our Bartholin glands (which are a pair of small glands located on either side of the labia, outside the opening of the vagina) secrete a lubricating fluid for the purpose of sex. In other words, if we're not aroused to the point of secretion, we're dry, and who wants that?

Hormonal imbalance – If you've been experiencing symptoms like vaginal dryness, weight gain, night sweats, anxiety, having an overload of stress, hair loss and/or infertility issues, you should see your doctor to discuss your symptoms, have a panel of lab work done and a vaginal exam to determine the exact cause. You could have a hormonal imbalance, which could cause:

- Irregular periods
- Hair loss
- Acne
- Weight gain

- Hot flashes
- Facial hair
- Painful intercourse which could stem from vaginal dryness

Hormonal imbalances can also be related to childbirth and breastfeeding.

Menopause (pre/post) – There are multiple symptoms associated with menopause, but post-menopausal women can also experience vaginal dryness due to the decrease in the hormone estrogen that causes the lining of the vaginal walls to become thin, dry and less elastic. When it comes to menopause, there are different approaches that you can try to combat the dry vagina so do your research to see what the best option is for you.

Surgeries – Pelvic surgery, ovary removal and post-cancer therapy can all be associated with this issue.

Medications – Anti-estrogen, allergy, cold medicine, blood pressure, sedatives, pain meds and birth control pills are all a few of the common agents that can lead to vaginal dryness.

Cigarette smoking – According to menopausenow.com, smoking cigarettes destroys estrogen levels, leading to vaginal dryness. At the same time, smoking decreases the blood flow to the tissues of the body, leading to vaginal atrophy (thinning of the vaginal walls). Some individuals may also experience dryness with marijuana use; go figure.

Alcohol use – Alcohol causes dehydration, so too much makes it more difficult to have a moist environment. At the same time, increased consumption can make it harder to achieve an orgasm (and we don't want that!). The bottom line is moderation and knowing that everyone is different; therefore, individuals may respond differently to alcohol use.

Caffeine – Avoid or limit caffeine consumption due to its diuretic effects, which thereby increase dryness in the vagina.

Douching/sprays – I know that many women use these as cleansing agents, but mild soap and water will do trick without changing the natural flora down there. Instead of trying to cover up the smell, go to the doctor to see what that unpleasant odor is stemming from.

At the same time, if there is an odor and no infection, you may want to take a look at your diet. There are some foods known to cause odor in the urine and vagina.

Some of these foods include:

- Asparagus
- Garlic
- Onions
- Excess protein
- Broccoli
- Coffee
- Dairy
- Fried foods

Not enough foods rich in phytoestrogens – Phytoestrogens are compounds found in plant-based foods, and if we have these in our diets, they will act like or mimic the estrogen in our bodies. So, this would be beneficial if the estrogen in your body is low due to hormone imbalance or if you're going through menopause. I've compiled some of these foods for quick reference.

Again, these are foods that can balance the estrogen levels naturally before opting for a prescription. Always check with your doctor before making a drastic change.

Phytoestrogenic Food List

Vegetables	Fruits	Nuts/Grains	Soy
Kale	Dried apricots	Flaxseed	Soybeans
Brussels sprouts	Dried dates	Walnuts	Tofu
Cabbage	Peaches	Pistachios	Soy milk
Cauliflower	Strawberries	Almonds	Miso paste
Collards	Blueberries	Wheat	Tempeh
Green beans	Cherries	Sunflower seeds	Soy sauce
Garlic	Pomegranates	Barley	
Corn	Apples	Oat	
Alfalfa sprouts	Grapes	Wheat germ	

Liquids: Olive oil Red wine   Bourbon   Beer

Herbs: Red clover Licorice root Hops

These are all foods to eat to increase vaginal lubrication, according to a study by the University of Toronto.

Chapter 11 - *Bednastics*

Sexual Positions That Enable Better Sex

Menses who? I'm so glad she's gone; I don't know what to do. Now I can enjoy sex anywhere, anyplace and anytime.

This section isn't like other books that recommend sexual positions. The inclusion of this section was meant to help readers with limitations, pain or whatever their medical diagnosis is, have great sex without pain. I've had pain for the last 36 years, and trying to have sex is horrible if you don't make modifications. These are just a few of the positions my husband and I use. Whether you include them or not, what's most important is that you communicate and take your time so that you can have an enjoyable sexual experience.

- **Navel-to-Navel** (Commonly referred to as missionary) – This position allows for better clitoral stimulation, encouraging an orgasm from the woman's perspective. If there's pain involved, it will be helpful for him to keep his torso suspended upward, working those triceps and deltoid muscles. If this position is difficult or painful, try it with a small or flatter pillow under the small of your back for support. At the same time, I've noticed that if I bend my legs, like in a frog's pose (keeping them on the bed) and have pillows supporting my legs on either side, I have no pain.

- **Back Doe Little Joe** – Imagine him holding you in his arms (your back to his chest) with both your legs bent in a fetal position. We both love the closeness of this position, as if the two of us were one (and we are). In this position, I don't experience any sharp pain because there is no separation, only a smooth sliding motion.

☼I like this position because I'm able to kiss the nape of her neck and her ears. I also love holding her breast, one of my favorite parts of her body.

- **Side Winder** – Coming out of Back Doe Little Joe, this is a marvelous position of sensation and comfort. From the above position, allow your leg to rest on his hip, while the other is bent in between his legs. However, take his bent leg and pull forward towards your vaginal area for stimulation.

This position allows both to have a visual of each other, maintains optimal feeling and prevents any injury; it's a win all the way around.

- **Hold on, I'm Cumming** – Same position as Back Doe Little Joe, but he leans or pulls slightly away from you, holding both breasts. That slight change in position allows for deeper penetration because as he's leaning back, he's also pushing his pelvis closer towards your vagina.

☀ Again, I love her breasts, so this is a win for me. But I can also manipulate the clitoris, and this makes her hot and steamy.

- **The Pin-down** – In this position you are lying on your stomach, and he's directly on top of you, back entry again (there's something to be said about that vaginal wall stimulation). His hands are on yours or directly by your side. When he wants to kiss you, he can just come down, allowing his chest wall to touch your moistened back. To really feel his thrusts, meet him with a booty bump. And if you want clitoral action, take your own hand and work it out.

For support, place a pillow under your stomach; it will align the spine reducing any back pain.

☀ There's nothing I don't like about this position because I'm literally all-in.

- **Face Off** (side-lying lateral position) – One of my favorites because I can look into his eyes as we kiss and make love. This is also a position that doesn't add any pressure to my back because my legs are wrapped around his waist; it's so comfortable.

For additional comfort and support, grab a pillow and position it behind the small of your back; this prevents or decreases the wiggle back and forth. Furthermore, an additional pillow under the hip or buttock (that's not touching the bed) will align your hips, preventing any trauma.

☼ I'm able to use both hands to cradle her butt, so I'm a happy camper.

- **Modified All-Fours** (I like this name better than Doggie Style) – In this position, the woman gets on all fours and scoots to the edge of the bed while he stands directly behind, pulling you in. This position is more comfortable than both being on the bed  because the tendency is to put pressure on the mid-back, creating strain. With him pulling you in, he's slightly lifting you up, allowing for a wonderful stretch; it's a win-win.

For clitoral stimulation, he can place his hands near your groin (rubbing your clitoris) as he pulls you in.

☼ I like this position because I get more traction because my feet are on the floor. This gives me the ability to have more control and to dicktate the force (nope, it's not spelled wrong).

- **69 is just fine** – Everyone is familiar with this position; however, if you suffer from any pain in the neck, it will cause more of a strain bobbing up and down, for obvious reasons. For myself, it takes the strain off my neck if he's on top, but it may be uncomfortable for an extended amount of time because in this position his legs are open like a frog. So invite him to stretch when you're stretching throughout the week so that this position won't pose a problem.

☼ I'm on top, and if I'm getting head, I'm alright!

- **Lateral 69** – In this position you both turn on your sides keeping, the 69 position. What makes this position comfortable is the obvious lying down, without any possible strain on your back or neck. To get in close proximity, the two of you must open your legs. If you have any problem  with back pain, position a pillow behind your back to maintain the position and prevent any strain.

⚬ The closer you are, the more comfortable this position will be and the more coochie will be in your mouth, I'm just saying.

- **Happy V** – This is also a lateral position, but your heads are at 12 o'clock and 3 o'clock, creating the shape of a V. In this position his legs are straight, but yours are straddled around his hips. The motion is created by using your legs to pull you in and away from him. The  woman is in control, so you determine how long the strokes are and how strong the force is. At the same time, he can even be slightly elevated on one arm for more leverage.

We both love this position because when we need a change, it's easy to come back to the Face Off position; we love to kiss. Also, the use of pillows behind your back will assist in decreasing any extra movements or jerking of the back.

🔅I like this position because I can see her boobs bounce when I thrust; men are visual.

- **Tabletop** – This can be done leaning over the kitchen counter or in the bathroom leaning over the sink. You don't always have to be on your backs in the Navel-to-Navel position, that's boring. Change it up and learn to have fun with your partner.

If you're familiar with the yoga pose Cat/Cow, this is a great time to activate and stretch your back muscles. He is again pulling you into him, making sure to keep your hips in alignment to prevent any possible stress on the back. Take your time with this position and create long, yet slow rhythmic moves; the sensation is amazing.

🔅Breast action view in the mirror; does it get any better? I remember this position during a Las Vegas trip where she put warm sudsy water from the tub, the warm sensation on my, well, you know. That honeypot puts me over the edge.

- **High Knees** – In this position, the woman is on the bottom with her knees extended, almost like a knee-to-chest yoga pose with your legs open. He climbs on top of you with his hands touching the bed, keeping his torso extended. Now, you can either hold your knees, or what I like to do is position my legs on either side of his torso and hold onto his waist to control the amount of pressure. You should not feel pain. If you do, STOP! All I can say about this position is, Let the Church Say, *Amen!*

☼ "Pop that coochie" are the only words that come to mind for this position.

- **Upside-down Frog Pose** – Now, if your legs are able to bend without discomfort, you go girl! I aspire to be that flexible. But as for me, I need a little assistance, and this is by way of two pillows, one on either side of my bent legs while laying on my back so that I don't experience any pain. He then assumes the Navel-to-Navel position.

Likewise, this is a good stretch for your inner thighs, groin and hips.

- **Slide, Slide, Slippidy Slide** – Just like the name implies, ride him for your pleasure from a chair, or it can be done straddling him on the bed; it can even happen on the toilet (no judgment). This is a great position because you control the pressure and angle. For more pressure to your clitoris, lean into him, meeting chest to chest. The friction is amazing, and this position allows you to climax easier (but only if it's comfortable, ladies). My husband loves when I ride him; it gives him somewhat of a break and makes him feel like the king he is.

☼ I'm completely submerged inside of her and the sensation is great.

- **Lap Dance** – In this position, you literally sit on his lap with your back to his chest. I've found that it is much easier to open your legs wide so that you can use your feet to push off the floor. There is no clitoral stimulation, so you have to work it out to climax – one of you, anyway. Take your hands and guide him, show him how you like it. No shame in wanting him to learn how to make you moan.

The good thing is that there's no pain in this position to any body parts.

- **The Aquapussy Experience** – if your tub is large enough, water therapy is a wonderful way to add your partner to the party, truly an amazing experience. Try adding some candles to create the mood and put on some music; it adds the perfect touch. Here are the steps:

  1. Straddle him, face front with your legs wrapped around him. If you have bubble bath, add that to the mix.
  2. Make sure you have a bathmat first, and then you can do the Modified All-Fours position with each of you holding onto the tub structure for security. Then work that thing out!
  3. Sit on his lap as he massages your body. He can glide you back and forth with ease since you're in water, and the soap also helps to create the sliding motion.

Images captured by Desirée Poole

Oral Sex

"Does he think you're a good kisser?" Why didn't I know Usher was talking about oral sex? I'm super slow. Anyway, are you asked to be the guest of honor more times than not? If so, you're in there. But if he's commented on your skills, take it from me, simply ask him how you can make it better. No teeth, just fancy mouth work will do. More importantly, do you like his skills? Honey, if he's not doing it right, tell him because how will he know otherwise?

Ultimately, what men want is to please their partner, so if they're not doing something right, there's no stroke to his ego, and trust me, he wants that vote of confidence. I just laughed as I was thinking of this. If my husband's tongue isn't in the right place, I simply move his head to the right spot. And when it's getting good, I hold his head for dear life until the explosion happens. If it's okay with him, it's more than okay for me.

To ensure that you don't have a crook in your neck hours after your sexual encounter, have an ample supply of pillows around you. Following are a couple of positions that I use to reduce or prevent neck pain. At the same time, while in position, rotate your head slowly from left to right; it prevents any stiffness. He won't truly know what you're doing because the change in movement will drive him nuts, thinking you brushed up on your skills.

The Praying Mantis – Both hands are opened wide, thumbs surrounding his penis while your arms are bent like a boomerang.

The Sleeping Woman – Your chest wall is on his leg and your head is resting on a pillow beside his head.

The Lazy Man – He's sitting either on the couch, a chair or the edge of the bed, while you're on your knees (supported on pillows). No neck strain is the name of this game.

These are just some of the positions that helped us have better sex, but it's good for couples to explore their own positions to see what makes them the most comfortable. Again, the most important thing is to just have fun in the process. Be creative and don't stop until you achieve success. If one position doesn't work for you, try another until both of you are happy and comfortable with the outcome.

For more excitement and enjoyment, change locations; don't get stuck to the bedroom only. Learn to break up the monotony. Break away from the routine positions and the language attached to the idea of making love. Learn to explore each other's bodies and minds on a regular basis; this is one of the ways you can bring the spice and fun back to the relationship. Moreover, talk about each other's needs on a regular basis because they are ever-changing.

Chapter 12 – *Heal Thyself*

Acknowledging Disappointments

Sometimes we can get into our own headspace about any negativity we think, feel or are experiencing in our bodies. This can have a negative impact on our sexual experience. When we're in this state, we believe that we're not fully equipped to handle what's before us, whatever the reason. It is important to know that even with our flaws, we are sufficient, we are necessary and that we are more than enough.

When you've gotten a handle on your feelings, you can then come up with a solid plan of action to tackle any problem. It's crucial, in this phase of acknowledgement, not to stay in that negative headspace. Try to tackle any issue head-on so that mental fatigue and/or depression doesn't take up residence.

When I was an active nurse, for any problem or disease process, I had to come up with a plan of care that fit each client's needs. Knowing that not all plans are suitable for every person was key. As things changed or progressed, so did that plan of care, and it needed to be tailored to the patient's needs. For example, a plan of care for a person with a diagnosis of pain would first need an assessment of the degree of pain.

Next, we would gather all necessary information by asking lots of questions and then put a tentative plan in place, understanding the person's ability to carry it out. Education would be the next step because the more a person knows about what they are experiencing the better they are able to handle it. After that plan is in place for some time, you would then need to measure its effectiveness. So, back to the care plan for pain.

Pain: Find out when the pain originated, to what degree, what the patient is taking to manage the pain, how often and what non-pharmacological agents they have tried: heat, ice etc. Follow up with regular teaching so that the patient/client is able to manage his or her own care plan.

Now, when we make a care plan for sexual health, we can follow the same idea or guide:

- First, identify the problem.
- What do they know about the diagnosis or deficiency?
- What have they tried and for how long?
- Have they seen a medical professional about this problem?
- Educate both parties.
- What do they know now about the problem?
- Are they following the plan of care?
- Is it working; has it been effective?

If the current plan of care is not working or effective, go back to the drawing board and come up with different ways of tackling the problem. The more both individuals are included in the care plan, the more effective and successful you will become in the management.

I think it's worthy of noting that you may not get the desired outcome you once had in mind, but supporting each other through the trial or hardship and acknowledging your feelings along the way is essential. Also, being consistent in communication will yield a stronger couple and success in the long run.

For my husband and me, the goal of course is love-making. Now, how we achieve this and the steps we may have to go through to get there takes patience, love and compassion on both parts. For us, it is not as simple every time as wham bam, thank you, ma'am. Again, for us, it may take preparation on some occasions, and that looks like a massage, hot bath perhaps, some cream for pain and/or oral medication.

At the same time, it may require an injection to make things happen; it's all about how you envision it or your perspective on the situation at hand. A negative thought will undoubtedly lead to or yield a negative result or outcome, but knowing that both individuals are all-in and that both individuals will do what's required to achieve favorable outcomes is always a WIN.

Let Go of Hurts and Forgive

If what's keeping you from an amazing sexual experience are past hurt(s), you may want to ask yourself what it is that's keeping you from forgiving them because part of the relationship is a sexual experience; it's innate. In other words, sex is going to happen whether you are part of the equation or not. If making love is not in the equation or at least on the table at this time, put everything on the line (with open communication) with sex being one of the goals, and the first on the list is **honesty**.

Being open and honest, giving yourself an opportunity to express yourself, takes courage, no doubt. Is the atmosphere one that is safe to be forthcoming? If not, why? You see, when there's an elephant in the room, you must acknowledge it; otherwise, it will ruin your relationship. Those things that we feel as if we cannot bring ourselves to discuss with others are obstacles in our path to a healthy relationship. You should be able to discuss any and everything with your partner. And if one of you is hitting a roadblock, it may be something that a third party can bring out so that the two of you are able to get back to the way it was when you met.

When communicating, be ready and open to receiving criticism. "Wait! I know you can't be talking about me! I don't do that!" Well, it's time to get those kinds of thoughts and language out of the picture because they will only lead to more negativity or "Stinking Thinking." Remember, hurt people hurt people, so be open and don't ever go out of your way to damage the relationship with your mate.

Because it's so easy to point the finger, it would be beneficial for the two of you to use I-statements. I-statements take the blame out of the equation and remove the finger-pointing. Instead, they help the person speaking to recognize their true feelings and to use those feelings as the basis for making legitimate statements.

For example:

"I hate when you yell at me, I'm sick and tired of it!" WRONG

CORRECT: "It makes me feel small when you raise your voice, and it doesn't allow me to hear you."

"You never help me around the house, and I'm tired of being your maid!" WRONG

CORRECT: "It makes me feel overwhelmed and underappreciated when I do most of the work."

I've been using this technique with our last two children, who are currently in the home; they bicker and blame each other all day, every day. Teaching them to use I-statements is actually beginning to help them communicate more effectively and get in tune with their own feelings at the same time. Just know that it takes work and practice to change your dialogue, so be patient.

Don't Emasculate Each Other

When you think of the word "emasculate," you often think of a woman's view of a man and the negative connotations therein – or is that just me? Truth be told, we can both emasculate each other and hold one another hostage, making one of us feel less than and/or inferior to the other. The definition of emasculate by Merriam-Webster is simply "to deprive of strength, vigor, or spirit; to weaken."

Now, this is easily done, especially when the conversation gets heated. When one person doesn't like what the other says, they tend to lash out with words of hatred or negativity, thereby turning the discussion into a game of tit for tat. Instead, at the opening of any conversation, lay down some ground rules. Write them down if you have to and post them on the wall. Some examples may look like:

Open with a word of prayer – Always bring God into the equation.

Speak the truth and always say it with love - Speak with compassion and work towards building each other up.

Always uses – Removes blame and shows empathy.

Keep consistent eye contact – Shows that you are listening.

Never give ultimatums – Remember you are on the same team.

Institute a cool-down period – Prevents a blow-up.

Reiterate what you think you heard – Removes confusion and demonstrates that you're listening.

Be realistic with requests – Only God works miracles; humans need time to change.

Be open to criticism – No one's perfect; take what you hear as being said out of love and know that change can strengthen the relationship.

Don't overdo it – Set a limit to prevent overload.

End with prayer – Thank God for the outcome and for the strength that's being built in the relationship.

Be Positive on Purpose (from the words of Bishop Keith Clark) and always be intentional with your words and actions. Every time a negative thought enters your mind, release it… it has no place or power in your life. Go out of your way to do and say things that positively impact your relationship. Set yourself up for success in and out of the bedroom.

Lastly, encourage one another and never rely on your feelings to be the indicator, having the final say. Allow your feelings to be only an indicator of a change that should be communicated to bring clarity and truth. When you allow or let your feelings dictate the situation, you run the risk of choosing wrong. Allow truth to dictate with concrete and transparent cues.

Educate Yourself

Education opens up our awareness; it strengthens and empowers, making us radiant beings. The more we know, the more we *glow*, thereby increasing knowledge to those around us, i.e., our children, co-workers, extended family and friends.

If your partner is suffering or stricken with a disease, educate yourself regarding their needs because it will only help the relationship in the long run. When we're kept in the dark and allow ourselves to be shut off from our significant other, we're actually weakening that invisible bond that holds us together. This, in turn, signals isolation and despair with the individual that's going through the trial. Whether it is pain, diabetes, fibromyalgia, or some form of sexual dysfunction, if they go through it alone, it makes them feel as if they are on a deserted island. But when we take part in their care and love them through it, we become a stronger team.

When my husband told me that he had a brain tumor (on our first date, by the way), my first inclination was not to worry because I knew that God would take care of him. We later found out that the tumor was benign (non-cancerous) and could really rest in peace. Thank You, Lord!

When he told me that he was a prostate cancer survivor and had to live with the side effects from surgery, I didn't worry. You see, when you truly love someone and are willing to be their ride-or-die, that kind of love wins every time. At the same time, if you're a believer, in the midst of tragedy, faith in God always triumphs over that crippling fear. I also had my nursing knowledge on my side and could draw from it, so I knew what I was getting into as well.

Well, as for me, the shit hit the fan so to speak, when I started going through my bout with chronic fatigue and increased pain (I had two surgeries within the first two years of our marriage, one taking place a few days after our wedding).

As if that wasn't enough, I'm also plagued with fibromyalgia that completely wreaks havoc on my entire body. Initially, the reality of my situation made me slip further into a depression, and this took me a few years to finally break free of. Just knowing and hearing the doctors say that there was nothing they could do to change my situation not only infuriated me but left me feeling hopeless. But, God!

God helped me to realize that I was looking at things all wrong. My husband is completely amazing; I think I've said that over and over again, but it's true. He helped me to focus on the *good* around me, and I can't say that those days were easy because they were far from it. Not knowing how my body would react on any given day made me miserable. Spending 90-95% of my days laying in the bed made me sick with fury, and in my eyes, what was there to be happy about when I felt as if I were being robbed of life as I knew it? But yet again, I had to look towards God. God's word completely changed my focus, and my husband was right there reinforcing it, a powerful tag-team that gave me hope.

Yes, my family was always there, but they didn't see my fragility day-in and day-out or the despair that was written on my face. They weren't there in the wee hours of the night when I couldn't help myself sit up on my own or get in and out of the bed. It was just the two of us, the majority of the time, when I couldn't make it to the bathroom independently because of the weakness or because the pain prevented me from doing so.

My husband educated himself as to what I needed. And when he didn't know what to do or say, he was right by my side praying and pulling me through. This is what a partner does, they help meet the needs of their team and never leave them feeling as if they have to do it alone.

So, what does this have anything to do with sex? Well, I'm glad you asked. Educating yourself regarding your own and your partner's health needs puts you in a position of power. It's foolish to think that sex won't enter the minds of either individual just because there's a health or medical issue on the table.

Sex is a part of life and a major factor in any relationship, so knowing what you can and can't do physically, understanding individual limits and creating a safe place for open communication are the first steps in allowing intimacy to move to the next phase.

The feelings or sexual appetite to be loved, touched and caressed are all a part of who we are; it's a part of our composition or make-up. So, if it is not possible to make love to your spouse without help, there are many helpful modalities out there. Vibrators, dildos, and clitoral stimulators aren't just for the woman to use on herself or by herself. There are some men out there who use vibrators to stroke the shafts of their penis and use vibrating rings as a way to add pleasure to the marital bed. These toys can help spice things up and consequently are and may be the missing link for some to solve the problem of penetration.

At the same time, if there's an inability and need to bring in adaptive equipment to allow making love possible, by all means, try various elements; go online to see what's available or perhaps go to your local adult store with your partner and ask questions. You may surprise yourself and enjoy bringing in sex toys/gadgets into the equation. There are tons of things that will facilitate making love possible and enjoyable.

You can also bring in extra pillows and use wedges or foam cushions that will assist in the alignment of the body, making love-making more comfortable. And surprisingly, there are specific chairs and lounges out there to support the body while making love. You can also explore adapted equipment for ADA use online.

When broaching the subject, ask questions to see how your partner feels about bringing things into the bedroom. Remember, use your I-statements to reduce any negativity or feelings of blame (i.e., "I'm not able to have an orgasm. What do you think about trying or adding a vibrator?" or, "I've noticed that you don't seem aroused during foreplay. What do you think about using a vibrating sleeve to add pleasure?")

So, take that trip to your local adult store; it just may be fun for each of you to pick out something that you would like to explore. Take this time to open up the dialogue and build the communication bond. The last part is the thrill, taking them home and letting the experiments begin. Have fun and enjoy your spouse in this magnificent, intimate way that God created.

Just a recap, this intimacy allows the release of those happy hormones that can, if nothing else, bring you a spot of joy, peace and comfort. Making love increases overall health, lowers blood pressure, increases libido, allows you to sleep better, decreases stress levels and so much more. So, don't wait for your relationship to hit an all-time low to try to fix it.

Begin the work at the onset of the relationship. And if you're deep into it and find yourself starting now, begin by opening up. Okay, your fragility is showing, but that's a great thing because it is there that honesty, truth and a deeper awareness take center stage. Be aware that just as making love takes two, well sometimes, both partners need to be completely vested to make a change and/or allow the awareness to happen. Remember, what God has joined together let no one come between, and that even means *you*. Work as a team to make your relationship stronger. Why not start now?

Keep the Fuse Lit and Never Let it Die

It may be hard to think in these terms, especially if you've been in the relationship for many years. At that point, we may think we know everything there is to know about our partner and what it takes to be the best version of ourselves. But we should keep learning and growing, not only for us but for the sake of the relationship.

What keeping the fuse lit means is that both individuals are making a conscious effort to be a part of each other's lives, every day. It's so easy to be distracted by the demands of life and forsake the needs of the person we're in a covenant relationship with. You may think that asking the person how their day has been is enough as you intersect and possibly collide at the front door. But before you know it, you end up strangers in the night, feeling lost and isolated, wondering if the relationship is going to make it.

Sadly, this is when one, if not both individuals begin to look outside of the relationship to fulfill their own needs. Now, I'm not talking about sexual intimacy, although this clearly happens in far too many relationships. But what I am referring to is a sense of fulfillment or validation that is needed on a regular basis, that, for whatever reason or whatever the circumstance, is not given because we think we have it all together.

What I've learned through the years is that people need varying degrees of affection and/or attention from their mates. That is why it is critical to communicate effectively, explore each other's needs and learn to pick up on their non-verbal cues consistently throughout the relationship. It's almost as if you're keeping a mental tab on your partner, listening, asking questions and giving feedback as you go.

Some people love or need that element of touch daily, while for others, it would be too much stimuli or sensory overload to hold hands, hug, or, as I've heard it called, engage in cup-caking each day. Get to know your partner (like you know your favorite song that you can sing without the lyrics posted in your face); know who you're working with so that you can be successful for the duration of the relationship.

At the very least, communicate, even if it's for 10 uninterrupted minutes (put your phones on silent), giving each other the decency to look into each other's eyes while openly sharing. This is one of the ways that you can keep the fuse lit in your relationship.

Sure, you may talk in passing, talk on the phone, talk while doing any number of things. But the difference is, you're actually saying without saying, you're important, that you care about your partner and the relationship. You're telling your spouse the relationship is valuable and worth it to you. Taking just 10 minutes a day will turn into more precious talking time, and of course, it can be done anywhere.

If you're not doing this already, start making him or her a priority and make them feel appreciated. Again, it's very easy to feel as if we don't have the extra time in the day to do this or to create an atmosphere of pleasure, especially if there are kids involved. But trust me, you can be creative and find ways to appreciate your spouse.

For example, I love eating rice (I used to cook it almost every night), always have, but my husband, on the other hand, loves eating potatoes. I remember him asking me, after a year or so into the relationship, "Babe, do you think we can have potatoes sometimes?" or he'd change the lingo at times and say, "I like potatoes too," as a way for me to remember and stop cooking rice all the darn time.

Well, there are times, either for breakfast or dinner, that I make my husband a potato dish, and he loves it. This is an appreciation chip in my favor. Likewise, if your mate likes taking baths, make them a bubble bath when they get home. Also, instead of having your usual dinner, order take out or switch things up and take them out. Again, showing appreciation is always the right call.

We can do simple things each day to elevate our mates, ourselves and the relationship in the process. When you're consistently adding valuable layers into the relationship, you end up producing a byproduct of love, hope and security that can't be matched.

The truth is, every day we grow and are learning or absorbing; therefore, we're ever-evolving. Motel 6's slogan is, "We'll keep the lights on for you." Be like-minded in love with your mate: always open in love, never closed off.

How can this be done? How can you keep the fuse lit in your relationship? Well, I'm so glad you asked. You keep the fuse lit by taking the necessary time out for each other. Just imagine a car running without gasoline or electrical currents; it can't be done. In order for any relationship to be successful, it takes input or an ongoing contribution. Well, the same is true for a plant to grow: it needs water and sunlight. So why should a relationship be any less needy?

Some think they can go for years and not add anything to their relationship. Sadly, these are the relationships that end in divorce or stay together for the kids, for finances or until one dies; real stuff. Some couples, after a few years, start wondering where they went wrong, why the fun fizzled or why they seem like perfect strangers. All because there was no cooking (work) going on. All relationships require work. If you leave a pot on the stove without monitoring it, it will burn. The same is true for any relationship. If you don't put in the work and necessary time for it to bloom, it will all come crashing down.

So here are a few examples of how you can keep the fuse lit in your relationship (try to find ways to be interactive):

- Go on walks
- Cook a meal together
- Travel
- Play boardgames or cards
- Do yardwork/gardening
- Go dancing
- Go on a double date
- Work out or take a fitness class
- Have sex
- Plan a long drive
- Go bowling

- Get a mani/pedi
- Go on a cookout
- Go shopping
- Do chores. Yes, chores, they have to be done anyway.

Aside from doing activities that require communication, you can also do fun things with your partner and have an amazing time without talking (i.e., going to the movies, watching television, playing video games, swimming, bike riding, getting a couple's massage). The most important thing is that you do it together, maintain consistency and have fun because these are the things that it will take to build a strong, healthy relationship, as well as ensure that you like each other in the next 20+ years.

Let Him Lead and Take Some of the Pressure off of You

In the beginning, the man dominated things and the woman was there to be his helper. I understand the "why" and the "how" things got misconstrued with the missing man, the drugs that have and will continue to run rampant in our communities, and/or families being created way too early and not having the ability to adapt in the mature sense. But the question is, how can we get back to basics without deconstructing the woman?

I think it's quite simple if we start our relationship out the right way, giving ourselves time to know each other, and if you're a believer, waiting on God to see if he or she is the correct match. At the same time, if we love, honor and don't emasculate our men, I believe it is possible for them to rise to the occasion and be all that God has created them to be.

Moreover, as the years progressed, women became just as educated as men. They soared when it came to various professions, and in some cases (or households), matched or even topped the man's salary. Well, this is still true today; women are as busy in the homes and just as busy in their fields, making it harder for her to find time for herself because she gives it all to her family, her job and the community she resides in.

Where's the balance anymore, that place that keeps us sane and on track, ready and eager to go the next day and onto the next phase in our lives? Can we get back there? What is it going to take to finally get us to that place and give the man his reign back?

I guess I'll start with the hardest word for some to wrap their heads around: Submission. I remember when my husband brought this scripture to me in the midst of company, in the backyard, for crying out loud. I mean, really, are you kidding me? That was my thought. I just left the Bible right on the table where he placed it.

At that point in my life, there was no way in hell that I was going to let anyone control or dictate things in my life. I had allowed my ex-husband to belittle and destroy my spirit and now that I finally found the voice I should have always had, I wasn't budging. I must say, it took me some time to get with the whole idea of submission. What did it mean and what place did it have in our home? Well, I guess, given the simple fact that I had married a minister, I was going to find out.

What my husband was trying to gently tell me, although it felt as if he was putting me on blast, was that there had to be order in our home. He's not one to argue but has no problem saying whatever enters his mind; there's absolutely no filter in his DNA. Me, on the other hand, I'm always ready to debate (I'm sure, because of my previous experiences), but I hadn't yet learned that this man wasn't going to hurt or harm me in any way.

There were things we had to learn individually; we had to wipe the slate clean of negativity and hurts from our past and understand that this was a new ballgame, one that was ordered by God. But what did order look like? As a child, my mother had always had the loudest voice in our home. What she said went, so I was literally at a loss. I didn't want to be controlled, overlooked or put on the back burner, so "submitting," in my eyes, wasn't going to work for me.

As time progressed, because it was a big deal to my husband, it was something I had to take a closer look at. And when he would say that he felt like a guest in our home, I knew things had to change. Order in the home to me is like a game of follow the leader. Outside the home and in every country, state and city, there are governing rules or laws that one must follow. Even drivers must follow rules to keep everyone inside and outside of the car safe, and when these guidelines aren't followed, there is chaos that at times is so severe it cannot be rectified. Order in the home is really no different; there is a hierarchy that should be recognized and followed.

Now, I in no way am saying that women shouldn't have a voice, that we shouldn't speak up for ourselves, be heard or have input. When it comes to marriage, a woman's voice was never meant to be silent but to be a helpmate. So, no, I am not saying that women should be quiet or silent in their relationship because that would be ridiculous. But what I am saying is that a wife should be supportive and loving. She should be kind and gentle and give her husband admiration.

Most are familiar with the scripture that says wives should submit to their husbands, but do we really know what it means? I like these versions better because they give you a more concise picture of what the Bible is saying:

Ephesians 5:22 NIRV, **Wives follow the lead of your own husband as you follow the Lord.**

And the same scripture, but a different version, MSG says, **Wives understand and support your husbands in ways that show your support for Christ.**

BINGO! What this scripture actually means is that a wife should trust that her husband will lead her and the family in the right direction. That the wife should love, respect and have her husband's back at all times. He's the quarterback designating the plays, understanding that there is no "I" in team but that it takes two or the whole team to accomplish a play.

Now, I must say that in order to lead, you must be qualified to hold the position. In other words, no man should expect his wife to follow him if he's arrogant and self-seeking, basically acting like a damn fool. Who wants to follow an asshole?

When it comes to submission and the wife, people get it all wrong, thinking that the woman is weak for conforming, but this is far from the truth. Following takes great restraint and strength. Following or carrying out a plan by someone you love means you're a team player; it means you are flexible and ready to work harmoniously.

Being a part of a team takes patience of course, but it also means that you are strong, courageous, confident, humble and committed to the cause. Love is at the very core of this kind of support and trust, or submission as some call it. This kind of love goes both ways, as the husband loves his wife, so much that he sacrifices himself to ensure the family unit is whole.

The husband, on the other hand, has the role of loving his wife just like Christ loves the church. When you have a two-way connection, the team is fortified and enabled; therefore, working as a cohesive unit. Okay, I know this subject may have been lengthy, but submission can be a touchy subject to some and thus required a bit more explanation. The last two things that, in my opinion, assist in giving the man his reign back are love and patience.

Love, we discussed earlier in the book, but what the word actually implies when giving the man his mojo back or giving him his rightful place in the relationship refers to a selfless kind of love. This love is what I call a can-do kind of love. This kind of love gives freely and offers without wanting anything in return. John 3:16 NIV explains it perfectly:

For God so loved the world that He gave His one and only son, that whoever believes in Him shall not perish but have eternal life.

We can all learn to love and give love unselfishly without wanting anything in return – a love that is thoughtful, kind and generous in all aspects.

Patience, on the other hand, is what some individuals lack but is totally achievable if given the time. First, a self-assessment should be done. Do not just think you have it in the bag, but ask yourself these questions to determine if you lack this much-needed quality:

- Do you find that you're short with people on a regular basis?

- Are you easily annoyed or angered?
- Do you lash out easily?
- Do you find that you can't seem to wait in most circumstances?

Think in terms of the long-term and not sporadic incidents. If you answered yes to any of these questions, you are probably an impatient person and could use some work in this area. The goal of course is to be happy with *you* but to also work harmoniously with your mate now and for years to come.

Isaiah 40:31 KJV, **But they that wait upon the Lord shall renew their strength; they shall mount up with wings as eagle; they shall run, and not be weary; and they shall walk and not faint.**

It's in the waiting that we gain strength, gain wisdom and thus learn patience.

Patience is determined by the ability to wait, to act or respond in a calm manner without fluster. A patient person does react but does so calmly with the ability of restraint without exaggeration or anger. For myself, I've always been known as a patient person, especially in the first four decades of my life. But, as the years have progressed, I've noticed that I have become less tolerant with certain people and situations that may arise.

I can honestly say that there are times that I feel the crazy lady coming out. It's in these moments that my husband is the symbol of peace and the voice of reason that can gently get me to realize that I'm on a 10 and need to bring it all the way down to zero. He'll come close to me and say, "Pray, babe." I thank God that these instances are few and far between. It's instances like those that allow me to know how truly blessed I am to have a God-fearing man, one who loves the Lord with his whole heart.

After those intense feelings, what allows me to see a different view is asking myself, was it really that bad? Or how could I have responded differently? More importantly, what in the world was going on, on the inside that would cause me to get so upset or react in such a way?

It's questions like these that reel me back in. The reality is that LIFE will happen, there will be people and situations that will try to elicit a negative response, but the simple fact is that we are the ones that hold the cards. We are the ones who can choose not to respond, but when we do, the response should be out of love and compassion.

Furthermore, the ability to wait or choosing to wait and not self-gratify or respond with extreme or a heightened sense of behavior can happen if we just image putting ourselves on pause. Replay the situation or conversation, take a series of slow, deep breaths and then choose to respond in love and not out of anger. If these things are done, patience will then emerge, and you will see life differently, or at least the people around you will.

All and all, patience really is a virtue, a wonderful quality to have. This is what I call "waiting without wailing." Instituting these qualities in your marriage – love, patience and submission – will only strengthen both individuals and allow the team to function the way God intended.

It's like a waterfall flowing downstream, hitting each curve, rippling off the rocks and later joining the main body of water. Can you picture its beauty? The sound, the splash, the tranquility, not to mention the color it produces. This is how your marriage will be displayed when all parts are working in harmony. This is why God made a couple because it takes two to make a thang go right!

Prayer

Thank You, mighty God, for filling me with Your goodness and granting me with the words that roam through the pages of this book. Thank You, God, for allowing love to come into my life, my heart, our house. God, You've completely changed my world, and I'm so thankful. Thank You for this book, God, and for the lives it will change because You ordered my steps. I even thank You for the heartache I endured over the years, because it allowed me to see the vast difference that four simple letters, l, o, v, e, can have in the lives of two people. So, I thank You for drying my tears, God. I thank You for comforting me through the fears, Lord, and turning my sadness into joy.

So now, God, I ask You to enter the hearts of Your people and allow them to truly know the kind of love that only You can give. Help each couple figure out their destiny or path that You've already laid out for them. Help them to not give up in the face of adversity but to be strong and courageous because in You is where they'll find the strength to continue their journey. Allow them to expose their vulnerabilities and truly open up. Help them to be able to communicate with their mate and share their deepest secrets and inner thoughts. Comfort the hearts of those in despair, those who are depressed and can't seem to find their way. Bless them now, mighty God, strengthen them and give them peace.

Father God, I ask that You bless the women reading this book to find hope and the desire to keep going. God, please allow them to see that who they are is in You. Please let the women reading this book know that they are loved and that they are beautiful, that they can do anything they set their mind to. Please allow my sisters not to depend on anyone other than You, God. Allow them to stand when they feel weak, allow them to stand, God, when they can't find their way, allow them to stand, God, when everyone has gone and the tears are falling, allow them the strength to just stand. Please allow them to hold their heads up and believe without a shadow of a doubt that they CAN. Help them to see who You really are and that they can do all things through You because You are where their strength comes from.

Thank You, Lord. Amen.

Blessed be the Lord, the God of Israel, from everlasting even to everlasting. And let all the people say, "Amen." Praise the Lord.

Psalms 106:48 AMP

God has spoken... And Let the Church Say, *Amen!*

Reference Page

5 Kegel Exercises for Women: Best Bets, Getting Started, and More. WebMD. (n.d.). https://www.webmd.com/women/kegel-exercises-women.

14 Powerful Herbs for Pain Relief That Could Help You. Pain Doctor. (2018, September 18). https://paindoctor.com/herbs-for-pain-relief/.

American Heart Association. (n.d.). http://www.AmericanHeartAssoc.com/.

Anderson, P. (2021, March 22). Psychology Today. https://www.psychologytoday.com/us/therapists/pamela-p-anderson-overland-park-ks/49778.

Arthritis Foundation | Symptoms Treatments | Prevention Tips | Pain Relief Advice. (n.d.). http://www.Arthritis.org/.

Beliefs and History of Faith in God and Jesus Christ. Christianity. (n.d.). http://www.Christianity.com/.

Best Pheromones for Men 2021. Phero Planet. (n.d.). https://www.pheroplanet.com/.

Better Health. (n.d.). https://www.betterhealthcc.org/.

Campbell, E. "I Love God"

Chapman, G. D. (2010). *The five love languages: how to express heartfelt commitment to your mate.* Manjul Pub.

Clark, K.L., World Assembly Family of Churches. Oakland, CA

Class 3 - Your Erogenous Zones. (2013, April 9). https://professsorwill.blogspot.com/2013/04/class-3-your-erogenous-zones.html.

Cole, N.K. (1954). "Smile." Capitol.

Common Facial Expressions and Their Meaning (with Pictures). EnkiVeryWell. (2019, April 4). https://www.enkiverywell.com/facial-expressions-list.html.

Cuncic, A. (n.d.). *Practicing Active Listening in Your Daily Conversations.* Verywell Mind. https://www.verywellmind.com/what-is-active-listening-3024343.

Davies, S. T. (2021, March 22). *Live Better, Work Smarter.* Sam Thomas Davies. http://www.samuelthomasdavies.com/.

Dictionary.com. (n.d.). Dictionary.com. http://www.dictionary.com/.

Domiano, P. (2019, February 9). *Bartholin Gland - Pictures, Location, Problems, Abscess and Inflammation.* Prime Health Channel. https://www.primehealthchannel.com/bartholin-gland-pictures-location-problems-abscess-and-inflammation.html.

Franklin, K. (2011). "Smile." Sony/Legacy.

Gray, J. (2012). *Men Are from Mars, Women Are from Venus: The Classic Guide to Understanding the Opposite Sex.* Harper.

Howard, M. (n.d.). Women's Health. https://www.womenshealthmag.com/.

Jakes, T. D. (n.d.). *How to Get Your Fight Back.*

Jensen, E. (2019, June 18). *6 Foods that Trigger Arthritis Pain.* Consumer Health Digest. https://www.consumerhealthdigest.com/joint-pain/6-foods-that-trigger-arthritis-pain.html.

Link, R. (2020, September 15). *Top 10 Pain-Triggering Foods.* Dr. Axe. https://draxe.com/nutrition/pain-triggering-foods/.

Love (noun). Oxford Advanced American Dictionary. (n.d.). https://www.oxfordlearnersdictionaries.com/us/definition/american_english/love_1.

Mayo Foundation for Medical Education and Research. (2020, December 4). *Vaginal dryness: Common and treatable.* Mayo Clinic. https://www.mayoclinic.org/symptoms/vaginal-dryness/basics/definition/sym-20151520.

Mayo Foundation for Medical Education and Research. (n.d.). Mayo Clinic. https://www.mayoclinic.org/.

Menopause Now. (2021, June 30). https://www.menopausenow.com/.

Merriam-Webster. (n.d.). *Dictionary by Merriam-Webster: America's most-trusted online dictionary.* Merriam-Webster. http://www.merriam-webster.com/.

MyBible Social App. My Bible. (n.d.). http://www.Mybible.com/.

Nelson, J. (2018, July 29). *A List of Emotions and Facial Expressions.* Thought Catalog. https://thoughtcatalog.com/january-nelson/2018/06/list-of-emotions/.

Pelvic Floor Muscle (Kegel) Exercises for Women. Memorial Sloan Kettering Cancer Center. (n.d.).

https://www.mskcc.org/cancer-care/patient-education/pelvic-floor-muscle-kegel-exercises-women.

Poole, Glyndelle. Personal Trainer, Train4Life Fitness.

Riggler, H. (n.d.). Grow in Faith with Daily Christian Living Articles. https://www.crosswalk.com/.

Smalls, C. (1978). "Slide Some Oil to Me," *The Wiz.*

Smith, S., & Welch, A. (2020, November 11). *Importance of Nonverbal Communication in Marriage & Relationships.* Marriage Advice - Expert Marriage Tips & Advice. https://www.marriage.com/advice/communication/nonverbal-communication-in-marriage/.

Step-by-Step Guide to Performing Kegel Exercises. Harvard Health. (2019, September 16). http://www.health.harvard.edu/bladdar-and-bowel/step-by-step-guide-to-performing-kegel-exercises.

Surgicaltechedu. (2018, March 22). *Prostatectomy - Surgical Tech.* Surgical Tech - A Career Guide for Surgical Technologists. https://surgicaltechedu.org/prostatectomy/.

Thought Catalog. (n.d.). http://www.Thoughtcatalog.com/.

U.S. Department of Health and Human Services. (n.d.). National Institutes of Health. https://www.nih.gov/.

Understanding the Teen Brain. Stanford Children's Health. (n.d.). https://www.stanfordchildrens.org/en/topic/default?id=understanding-the-teen-brain-1-3051.

University of Toronto. (n.d.). *Phytoestrogen Content of Foods Consumed in Canada, Including Isoflavones, Lignans, and Coumestan.* ResearchGate. https://www.researchgate.net/publication/6888063_Phytoes

trogen_Content_of_Foods_Consumed_in_Canada_Including _Isoflavones_Lignans_and_Coumestan.

WebMD. (2020, August 11). *10 Foods That Fight Pain*. WebMD. https://www.webmd.com/pain-management/ss/slideshow-foods-fight-pain.

Westheimer, D. R. (2018, April 5). *Ask Dr. Ruth: Can Kegels Make Sex Better?* Time. https://time.com/5228035/dr-ruth-kegels-benefit-sex-life/.

What Are the Side Effects of Marijuana? Drugs.com. (n.d.). https://www.drugs.com/medical-answers/side-effects-weed-3453651/#:~:text=Official%20Answer-,by%20Drugs.com,some%20impairment%20in%20respiratory%20function.

Wikimedia Foundation. (2021, April 17). *Foreplay*. Wikipedia. https://en.wikipedia.org/wiki/Foreplay.

Zavada, J. (n.d.). *What Kind of Biblical Love Is Eros?* Learn Religions. https://www.learnreligions.com/what-is-eros-love-700682.

About the Author

Everything she's gone through in life has prepared her for this very moment. When tragedy hit, she rose to the occasion to rediscover herself. So, who is she? Sabrina Washington grew up in San Francisco, later migrated to Oakland, CA, and now resides in the Central Valley. She is an amazing wife and mother of eight, grandmother of nine, she's rocking life to the fullest with her man by her side, she can't lose. She holds a BSN from USF but her highest honor is wife, mother and child of the King, and she wears her medal proudly. At age 52, she's just beginning to let the world know who she is. So, get ready because she's risen from the ashes and is currently blowing across this planet like wildfire.

Made in the USA
Columbia, SC
13 November 2021

48873975R00117